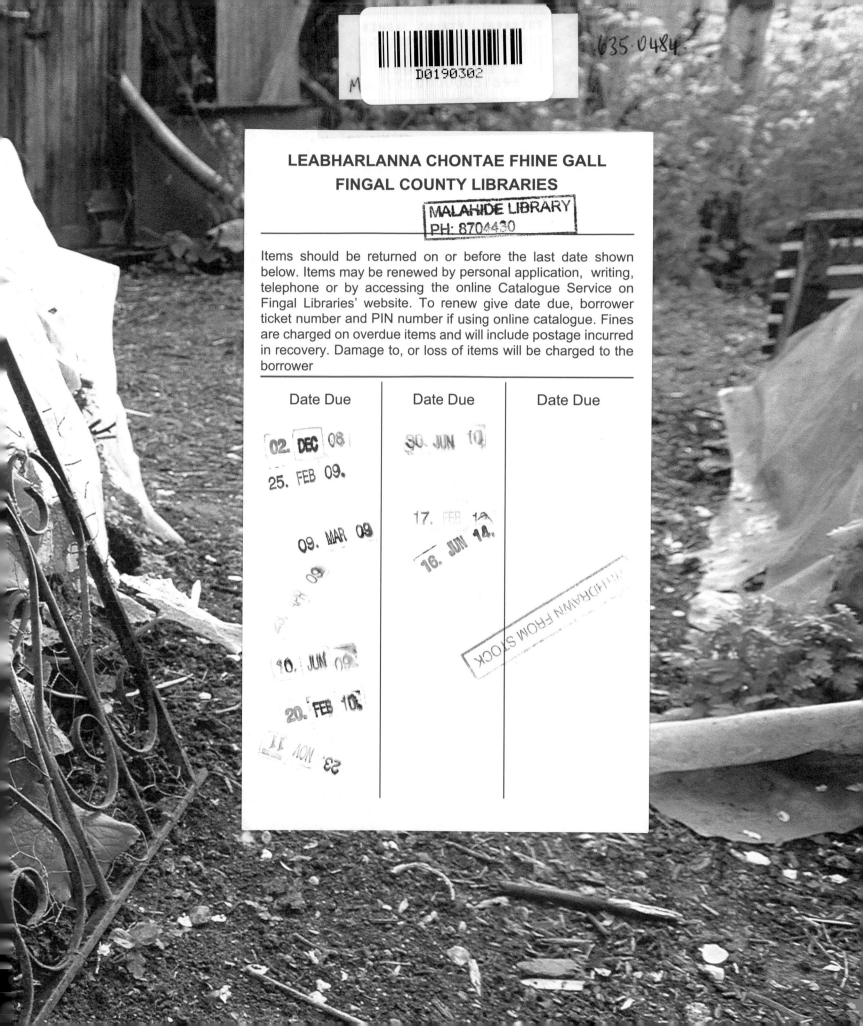

grow your own
eat your own

grow your own eat your own

BOB FLOWERDEW'S GUIDE TO MAKING THE MOST
OF YOUR GARDEN PRODUCE ALL YEAR ROUND

photography by peter cassidy

KYLE CATHIE LIMITED

DEDICATION

To their mother Vonnetta and their Godmother
Tracey Mobbs: many many thanks for keeping my
two year-old twins, Malachi and Italia, out of my hair
just long enough to get the work done.

First published in Great Britain in 2008 by

Kyle Cathie Limited
122 Arlington Road
London NW1 7HP

general.enquiries@kyle-cathie.com

www.kylecathie.com

ISBN 978 1 85626 787 8

Project editor Sophie Allen
Designed by Nicky Collings
Photography by Peter Cassidy
Home economy by Lizzie Harris/Bob Flowerdew
Styling by Wei Tang
Copy edited by Penny Phillips
Production by Sha Huxtable

A Cataloguing in Publication record for this title
is available from the British Library.

Printed and bound in China

contents

Introduction

It's easy to produce this or that fruit or vegetable for fun or for the table, each in its due season. But one day you realise that most crops in the garden only arrive once, are in glut 'now', with no more to be had for another year – unless you do something about it. This book is about how to get the best value, throughout more of the year, from your produce, and how to adjust and order your harvests so your crops flow smoothly to fill your stores and pantry. And how lucky and fortunate gluts can be, when easily processed, so they find their way onto your table most enjoyably.

Eating in season is good, and healthy, and growing your own is about raising the quality of more of what you eat. But as you grow to fill your home delicatessen you need to adjust your growing methods to match. You see, eating in season is about having a little every day. Growing for processing is more at one go. Anyway, when eating in season you have different fresh items much of the year – but you still need other things, out of season, to go with those. In any meal we usually have several small amounts of many crops, such as herbs or say onions, as well as actual portions of others, say potatoes. To provide every one of these 'fresh' would be incredibly difficult for much of the year for any individual. (It's not the ease, skill or desire, of course, but the time and effort and thus would be quite achievable by a larger establishment with more labour and resources.) Anyway, to insist on having every item absolutely fresh every day would be a bit pointless if many are going to be cooked. It simply makes sense to store and preserve as much as you can in season of your own home-grown produce to keep you provided as long as possible after your fresh supplies run out. And if you believe in eating what you have rather than what you fancy so the more available ingredients the better. With more fresh, stored and processed ingredients, the more possible recipes and the finer your table. And that more mundane point – you've got a glut so here's what's best do with it!

Matching production
to the kitchen

Matching production to the kitchen

GLUTS: THEIR USE... AND HOW TO AVOID TOO MUCH OF A GOOD THING

Gardening is inherently risky. Weather has more to do with success or failure than we appreciate. The wrong weather at a crucial time – be it frost, hail, drought, searing wind or scorching sun – can halve our crop or wipe it all out. Just a small change can affect some crops – for example, I've recently experienced more difficulty growing outdoor tomatoes than I did twenty years ago, even with the same varieties, simply because of greyer, damper summers. Some years are good for one crop and bad for others – but the problem can be just getting any crop at all. Then, occasionally, because you have allowed, as the old sowing adage goes, 'one for the birds, one for God, one for the weather and one for yourself', you end up with a huge glut. A 'glut': more than you can normally use.

Obviously planning what you sow and grow each year can help reduce gluts, but you need to be ready. You may get a huge crop and then, because you don't decide quickly enough what to do, lose it all – watch the whole lot go over, even before you can give it away. The trick is to see it coming, make plans and be ready to take advantage of such a blessing. So if your peas or beans start to throw huge crops as conditions favour them, be prepared: process them before they coarsen, to cover not just this year's consumption, but next year's too. Plan also when to do so, as most crops are perfect for only a small window of time.

Another example is plums, which are notorious: for years you get nothing and then, because there are no late frosts, you get a huge crop and they break their branches. Knowing this, you can thin the crop earlier when you see the congestion and thus save the branches – and reduce the glut to more manageable proportions for processing. And then you can store the surplus plums in all sorts of ways to cover the next few 'off' years.

Or maybe you have an apple tree that crops really heavily one year, then produces none the next year, followed by a glut again, and so on. This is what is termed biennial bearing – it's like getting exhausted, taking a holiday and then working flat out again. The answer is to thin the crop heavily in the 'on' year while the fruits are still small; this reduces the strain and you get a crop both this year and the next – when you also thin heavily, and so on.

Don't forget: thinning fruits nearly always gives you the same weight of crop in the end but in fewer, bigger, cleaner examples, thus saving you a lot of picking, processing and handling. Thinning also reduces pests and diseases, as obviously any infested or infected fruits are the ones you remove first. But most importantly it replaces an unmanageable half-spoilt glut every other year with a convenient number of more attractive fruits every year.

MORE CONTINUOUS PRODUCTION: EXTENDING YOUR HARVEST

Avoiding gluts beyond your capacity to handle them is an important goal; there is no use having the stuff if you can't deal with it before it goes off. However, you do want manageable gluts: small surplus quantities produced beyond your weekly needs; and crops produced over longer periods, so that you consume more fresh and have more options about when to deal with any surplus.

Gardeners may need to grow with slightly different approaches, depending on how they intend to consume their crops. Eating in season is the simplest: when you've grown it, you eat it. The season can be extended for some vegetable crops by sowing and planting in consecutive smaller batches, to give many smaller harvests throughout more of the crops' natural season. However, the growing season is clearly not the cropping season – things have to grow first! – and the bulk of production tends to come in summer and early autumn. Most gardens are thus generally shortest of fresh variety from midwinter till late spring, and it's early summer before you get any surpluses of much at all.

Still, with a bit of planning and effort you can harvest many crops, mostly salads and herbs, almost all year round. As well as starting off earlier with the earliest (quickest) varieties, and making sowings for longer, you can have much later crops, too, by growing late-maturing main-crop varieties. Where you have late varieties for storing you can get virtually year-round supplies.

PAGES 10–11 A two tier, or is it two tyre, strawberry bed produces more than on the flat.
LEFT Poor goose – she can't cope with all those apples on her own! (Tubs have citrus trees in them put out for the summer.)

Concentrate

This is where you start to change your gardening methods. In order to put aside enough crop, and to process that quantity, you will probably want to grow fewer small batches than you would to provide your more regular supply. Inevitably you'll start growing larger and larger batches with the aim of processing and clearing a whole load at one go – over one weekend, say. Few of us are dedicated enough to grow and store everything, so most of us will be growing, storing and processing just a few really important, or easy, crops – relatively huge amounts of one or two favourites. Look at most allotments: you can tell those of the old hands by how few crops there are, and those of the novices by the sheer variety they are trying. The old hands concentrate on the crops and the varieties they know do well; they grow just those they've found worth the effort. But of these they'll grow loads, and harvest and process them in bulk – sometimes with the whole family helping, as in earlier more rural generations.

Of course, you don't have to go for a factory-scale operation, or even do big batches. It is quite possible to set aside just a little every day, processing or part-processing extra portions before each meal, and just popping these in the freezer or putting them aside to dry. If you pick, say, French beans a couple of times a week for meals, then processing and dealing with a few extra is little effort and you can soon accumulate a quantity. With some crops or methods, on the other hand, processing is better done with a big batch or several – especially when, for example, brining and pickling or brewing is involved.

Fortunately these approaches are not exclusive – you don't have to choose one or the other. In practice you can often have half a dozen things going on at different stages all at one time, with some batches being processed – say, juiced or jammed – alongside small portions being 'salted' away or, more likely, dried or frozen. And don't forget to keep using all those things you are preserving. Keep going through all your stores – remove the too long gone, give away any surplus and use the best yourself, now.

The annual cycle

Along with temporary gluts and long famines that need bridging, there is the annual problem of providing as much as possible over as long a period as possible, when most crops naturally harvest over a short period. With all the skill and effort outlined above it is possible to force earlier crops, hold some back and store many fresh in the ground. But a great many are onerous to grow out of season and decay so quickly that they need to be processed immediately to be kept at all – especially relevant if they're a valuable glut you don't want to waste.

Raspberries are a good example: fresh they can be grown productively outdoors in only two bursts, midsummer and autumn; under cover or out of season they are very difficult and subject to too many problems. So they need to be frozen, jammed, juiced and so on, as soon as they can be picked and before they rot – which for a damp, ripe raspberry seems to take but a matter of minutes!

However, notwithstanding such difficulties and with incredible inputs and dedication people have somehow grown almost anything every month of the year. Queen Victoria's gardeners were expected to produce four pounds (two kilos) of ripe strawberries at short notice and on any day of the year – along with box-loads of fresh grapes and pineapples. (Of course, they did have magnificent resources and steam-powered hothouses.) Only a very few edible things can be easily grown outdoors all year round; naturally these are nearly all salady, herby and spinach-type leaves or roots. And, unprotected from the weather, even most of these are not very palatable – and if low-growing nearly always mud-besplattered.

OPPOSITE PAGE If the two apples at the top had been thinned to one in time, then it would now be as big as the well spaced lower fruit.

BELOW Rocket and Miners lettuce are allowed to self-seed along the side of the path (a recycled radiator panel) where they are always handy.

RIGHT Grape vines are well worth growing in tubs to force under cover – and they don't have to grow alone – strawberries work well as they're now out of reach of slugs and weeks ahead of outdoors.

REGENT

From spring till autumn, almost everything that is commonly grown can be chosen to be an early, main or late-cropping variety, giving you the longest season subdivided into smaller batches to spread production more continuously. Everything can be started sooner by beginning growth under cover and then putting plants out later – they'll already be bigger than those started outdoors – or you can buy in ready-to-put-out plants, but growing your own gives a better choice of variety. In either case the crucial thing is to acclimatise the plants to the new conditions by hardening them off before you plant them out. Move them outdoors in the day and keep them under cover at night for a week or so – longer if it's very cold – and don't plant them out if they are tender and frost is still likely.

We spend a lot of time and effort getting earlier crops; however, we also need to consider the other end of the harvest, and good storage depends on well-grown late crops. You can start to do this by sowing in small pots, or in multi-celled trays, and then as one crop is removed from the garden a young seedling can be popped in its place. As you go through each tray, the seedlings will be transplanted at different times, the later ones getting more of a check. Or you can hold back half a row of lettuce, cabbage or some salads by lifting alternate plants and immediately replanting them in the same place; this makes them mature a week or two later than those left alone. (Sadly, if this is done badly – too late, or in hot, dry, conditions without watering – it may make them bolt, which is of little use.)

An often unintentional way of holding back some crops, such as tomatoes, peppers and cucurbits, is to leave ripe fruits on the plant; this suppresses more forming while the existing crop's maturing and ripening continues. This is usually inconvenient – a tomato may ripen up best on the plant, but if left there will reduce the total crop, whereas if it's picked and ripened separately the crop will be sooner and bigger. This effect is most pronounced with courgettes and cucumbers, where one missed fruit swelling up and yellowing will stop all others forming; if production suddenly halts for no reason, search for that ripe fruit and remove it! Likewise if one sweet-pea or French-bean pod is allowed to ripen its seeds, few more are produced. Regular careful inspection is essential for keeping up the output. Likewise any plants bolting (flowering and running to seed early) should be removed before they encourage others.

If the tougher crops are grown in autumn, many will stand under cover of a cloche or plastic fleece and be available in winter. And given some good glass or plastic cover, it's possible to have crops – mostly saladings, Chinese greens, herbs and spinaches,

radishes, spring onions – truly fresh twelve months a year. For winter these are best started in a warmed propagator in small pots or cells and planted out, preferably in big pots on the staging rather than down in the border. Giving them warmth helps, but more light will help even more, as their biggest enemy is damp moulds when they are not growing strongly. A few really fresh crops are achievable in midwinter if you use a bit of cunning. With warmth you can force roots of asparagus, seakale, chicory, dandelion and rhubarb to shoot. Grow these as plants the previous summer specifically to force out of season. Pack their roots in damp sand and little more is required, as the shoots you want come from the existing materials in the roots. These roots require only dark warmth, so pots of them can be stood in a cupboard in a black bin bag rather than taking up valuable greenhouse space.

Fresh fruit is more difficult to provide all year round. By growing on the sunny and shady sides of a wall you can extend the season of most by a week or maybe a few, and with suitable early and late varieties add another month or two more. But really out-of-season fruit may involve a lot more skill, and luck. Fruit, being mostly perennial, is much more governed by the changing seasons, and 'knows' it needs to stay in synch. (That is why it is so hard to crop olives, loquats, even citrus outdoors in temperate climates such as in the UK – these want to set and swell crops through a milder winter, with ripening coming with the next batch of flowers.) However, with a frost-free glasshouse you can easily have fresh citrus, tree tomatoes, hot peppers, guavas and even pineapples in winter when other fresh fruit crops are less available.

Growing fruits under cover all the time may lead to massive pests and disease problems, and lack of dormancy. One answer is to modify Rivers's old orchard-house method. This involves moving pot-grown fruit trees and bushes under glass/plastic to force them into earlier growth and much earlier, more certain harvests. This, together with holding others back in cold places, makes it possible to have some fruits – especially such as grapes and lemons – for three parts, if not all, of the year. It becomes easier still with more heat, and with extra light and or artificial day-lengths; then almost anything becomes achievable – if it's really wanted. Tomatoes, strawberries and cucumbers, as well as many other crops, could be provided every day of the year. But this is not easy without huge expenditures in labour and energy; it is probably better to go for the easier options and store and process more.

OPPOSITE PAGE Start onion sets off in cells and plant out for reliably early crops.
THIS PAGE Strawberry guavas (below) are healthy, tasty and as hardy as citrus (above) – that is not very hardy at all – but well worth having in a frost-free greenhouse for their out-of-season crops.

GROWING FOR STORAGE

Storage is another option if you want to eat virtually fresh-grown and fresh-picked, as many crops stay fairly fresh for a while once harvested. You can have potatoes all year round from those just dug and those stored – but probably not the same variety. Growing more crops for storage will probably include a change in or addition to the varieties grown for eating in season, as some sorts are far better than others. With the right apples well stored, this fruit can easily be had fresh for three quarters, if not the whole, of the year. It is hard to extend the fresh season of many other tree fruits by as much as apples, as most others – save the nuts – store poorly by comparison. Indeed, old apple varieties existed that apparently kept for two years or more (handy for long voyages but not reckoned awfully palatable). On a more enjoyable scale, the earliest apples ripen in summer, and the late ripeners – picked when the frosts and birds are too damaging – are, with a bit of simple storage, good through winter and into spring.

My favourite storage aid is a dead fridge or chest freezer. Neat, tidy and with thick insulation and a rodent-proof skin, these make very good stores. I damage the rubber seal to let in some air – but not with holes big enough to let in mice. With a couple of these units in a shed, crops like apples, cabbages, carrots and other roots, potatoes, even pumpkins and squashes and so on, can be kept in good condition – as good as in a traditional root cellar or clamp, and with easier access. Don't pack your produce in paper bags, as these fall to bits, as do paper labels; use plastic bags, baskets or buckets in the humid conditions of a root or apple store.

Choosing the right varieties

Good storage is often about choosing the right varieties and growing them as late in the season as possible, and as well as possible – that is, without damage. Specific varieties are known to store well, and these are the only sensible ones to store; any others are probably better processed in some way. But more importantly – only ever try to store a crop if it is in first-class condition. If a crop has any damage, or there is any other reason why it may not store, then it's better to process it before it becomes worthless. If you wish to store anything, it must be close to perfect – no holes, rots or bruises. If just one item in ten rots every month, then to have a tray of apples or a bag of potatoes to use in six months' time you must set aside two now.

(The maths bit, in case you are curious: if you put 100 fruits or roots aside in perfect condition, and one in ten rots each month, then after one month there are $100 - 10 = 90$; after two months, 90 $- 9 = 81$; after three, $81 - 8 = 73$; after four, $73 - 7 = 66$; after five, $66 - 7 = 59$; and by the end of the sixth month the 100 will have shrunk by almost half, with only $59 - 6 = 53$ left.) And in practice, the rate of deterioration increases during those final months, so to have a box every month for longer than the first few months becomes increasingly difficult. Just to get you through six months you need not six but maybe nine, ten or even a dozen boxes at the start. And all in perfect condition. Of course, if you want to store them for only a short while, they still need to be in fair condition or they may go off anyway. If in doubt, process a crop in some way before it goes over, rather than lose it to the compost heap – and as a backstop there is the chicken, egg and meat route (feed any surplus to the chickens and recoup it later), which adds a whole new world to your grow-it-yourself delicatessen.

Along with choosing the right varieties for storage is growing them well: growing not only with no flaw or blemish to hinder storage but also with a high dry-matter content, a thick skin and a resistance to rot. These qualities are obtained by your growing the plants with plentiful (but not excessive) moisture, plenty of sun, and not too much fertility – though plenty of potash, preferably from wood ashes. Plenty of organic matter in the soil or compost is crucial, especially for potatoes. For processing, the quality of the flesh is paramount, but minor blemishes are not generally a problem, whereas for storage even the most minor damage may be fatal; thus stored crops need more pest and disease protection than crops grown to eat fresh or for processing.

Harvesting is also a critical stage as far as storage is concerned, as only the finest and most perfect should be selected – which rather conflicts with harvest's being left as late as possible. Most crops for storage need to be taken in as late as possible, but not all – pears, for example, are picked early. For all harvesting, choosing a dry day is important, as is a bright day to aid inspection and remove pests or soil. Whereas crops for processing need to be dealt with straight away, crops for storing may be moved out of the weather and cured, allowing the air to thicken the skin of some, or to dry others out a bit, before they are packed away.

Keeping records of the stored crops

Storage is usually outside the kitchen, so it helps to have a list of what is growing where, and what has been put where, so you know what is available for use in the kitchen and where to find it.

RIGHT **A card index, with each card a plan of the bed that year, ensures if labels are lost you still know which variety is where.**

Indeed it helps also to have a reminder list of what is available right now fresh in the garden, and a list of other stores, such as roots, apples and the contents of the deep freezer. Keep a note of what is running low or is needed, and keep a diary of sowings, plantings and new stock or seed to be bought – to be entered as soon as thought of. And also take note of what you don't use, as there is little point growing and storing more!

It is unlikely you will keep any 'fresh' stores into a second year; however, it is very likely you will carry some processed and preserved stores for much, much longer. Some wines acquire virtue with age. However, most things are not as nutritious or tasty as they age, no matter how well treated. So whereas in a commercial operation it is 'first in, first out' so as to keep the stock moving, for home consumption the opposite may be better. Always use the youngest first unless vintage is required. This year's jams, pickles, juices and leather, dried and frozen foods are probably far better than last year's. So use up the freshest first and then work backwards, if forced, into older stock.

With little effort I have built up a massive back selection. Since I've always made – by a small amount – more jams and pickles than I consume, the build-up has been a continual trickle. Just a couple of jars of this, a couple of that – and over decades I've accumulated a vast supply. Handy for the next famine but not for the current table – although interesting from an experimentation angle. I can personally vouch that few comestibles are better for becoming older, save some jams, wines and bay leaves.

The point is this: if you are not in a survivalist situation, eat the last in first and do not use the older ones until necessary. This applies to almost everything and especially to frozen items. Most importantly, try to avoid that odd habit of frantically using up everything frozen from last year to make space for everything being frozen now. Even though it seems a waste, eat the fresh if it is available – even if, to make the space, you have to give away last year's frozen items to friends. (Or to the hens.)

And occasionally add to those put-away survivalist stores any bought-in products – herbs, spices and so on – more than a decade past their sell-by date. You really don't want to use them, do you? Go on – sort them all out and get some fresh replacements; there's no point growing exquisite foods to ruin them with stale or rancid flavours.

RIGHT Fleece and fine netting covers keep flying and crawling pests away, giving superb low-labour protection and much cleaner crops.

GROWING FOR PROCESSING AND PRESERVING

When you consider this, rather than growing for fresh consumption or for storage, it may dictate another change in or addition to the varieties you grow. There are strawberries that keep their texture better after freezing than do others, plums that are best for prunes, and no end of vegetables selected for freezing, or drying well – even potatoes that make for crisps retaining the least oil ('Record').

You almost certainly will want different varieties if you want to process in batches. Most F1 varieties have been bred for field-scale cropping where all mature together, so for batch processing they are well suited. Old varieties often mature unevenly and over a longer period, so are more suited to being eaten fresh in season when you want to have some every few days over several weeks.

But more than the varieties, you may need to vary your methods. For fresh use, the blemishes and rots are annoying but almost irrelevant – especially if the produce is to be peeled and cooked – but with stored crops, such flaws are disastrous. A few faults may adversely affect processing – though fortunately most often it's merely something that needs cleaning out. If the crop is to be processed, most minor pest and disease damage really is irrelevant unless it will cause too much extra work, whereas for storage such damage would be unacceptable. Employing horticultural fleeces, nets and plastic barriers will stop most problems and should be used just in case anyway. For processing you may want to grow more plants closer together to give mini, smaller-size crops, such as baby carrots for freezing, rather than big ones grown far apart for storing.

Your methods of treatment may also vary: plants producing crops for freezing need to be grown differently from those for drying – the former needing to be more succulent, the latter more solid with a higher dry-matter content. Fruits, such as apples, for storage need a low-water, low-nitrogen, high-potash regime, whereas for fresh use and a crisper apple they may like more water and nitrogen. For jamming, crops such as strawberries are better grown drier in full sun than moist in part shade, yet the latter will have the better fresh flavour. Carrots for freezing need to be succulent with thin skins, so should be grown fast and moist, while for storing you want them big, solid and with thick skins, so grow them more slowly in less moist soils.

For drying uses, plants do not need to have it dry: too dry conditions give too solid a texture. A high dry-matter content is good, as too much water makes for more rots and slower drying, but even so, a vegetable grown with sufficient water is much better textured and milder flavoured than one grown in the dry –

OPPOSITE PAGE **Superb pears, 'Doyenne du Comice', deserve individual wrapping – but exposed enough to see when they ripen and colour.**

even though the latter may have a very high dry-matter content. So well-grown succulent carrots well dried will be noticeably sweeter and less tough when reconstituted than dry grown carrots equally well treated.

HARVESTING CROPS FOR DIFFERENT USES

Crops eaten fresh are often taken at a different time from those required for storage, or for processing. And for processing there is only one general rule: most vegetables for pickling or freezing are better taken on the young side; and the same generally – but not always – goes for fruits for jam or juicing.

Fruits

Eaten fresh, most fruits are best fully ripe, though a few are better just under-ripe and some, like melons, may be preferred overripe. For storing, perfection is required, and very few fruits store fresh for very long at all. Just laid on trays of shredded paper in a cool airy place, many fruits will do better than in the fridge, which chills them. Laying them on shredded paper allows them to breathe and stops there being a hard spot or bruising. The ideal alternative is to suspend fruits on or in a soft net or cloth, held on a frame, allowing air all over with no pressure points. The best chances of success are with pristine, not-quite-ripe dry fruits untouched – remove and handle them by their stalks, and the twigs they were attached by, and then clip them by these with clothes pegs to lines. These can be kept for relatively long times if in cool, almost dry, dark places.

Surprisingly, redcurrants were commonly simply placed fresh in jars and stored in the cool for winter pick-me-ups. Grapes were once sealed in pots of dry sawdust, which were covered in pitch and lowered into wells and ponds; on their recovery months later, the grapes were fine, but would last but a day. (One recalls myths of feasts that were all rotted the next morning being regarded as magic; now we understand that was because the Greek adventurers were ignorant of the finer arts of horticulture and domestic economy and did not understand how amazing, out-of-season delights had been procured for them.)

It need not be said that only picked fruit should be stored; windfalls are bruised and do not keep even if apparently clean and uncontaminated, and should be processed or used quickly before their condition deteriorates. Another minor point to watch is that the very earliest fruits to ripen are frequently infested with some bug and are often best picked and promptly used or processed rather than left to re-infest.

Herbs

Most herbs are at their tastiest just before they flower; many become bitter or hot with flowering, and although some annuals can be cut back to get a new flush of leaves, it is often better to start a new batch. Hot, dry conditions suit most perennial herbs, but those such as chives and annuals grown for their fresh rather than dried leaves definitely need moister conditions. None of the herbs ever wants feeding unless it has been starved in a pot, neither for fresh use, nor for storing or preserving do you want rank soft growth. And few are much value – not even mint – when grown in shade, though a little part-shade is not so much of a problem.

Although most herbs are grown for their leaves, the majority have edible flowers which can be used in addition. It is said that the best time to harvest most herbs is early in the morning, as soon as the dew has dried, though they can be picked almost any time that's convenient (but, obviously, after a hot dry afternoon much of their tasty pong will have gone). And as herbs rely on volatile oils, it is most important to dry them in cool, airy – but not draughty – positions, not to expose them to undue heat for any time, and to seal them away in the dark and cool. Those that are frozen must be similarly well sealed to prevent their smell from evaporating away.

Salad crops

Saladings are similar to herbs in most ways, though fewer are any use once flowering commences – although, of course, as with herbs, sometimes the flowers are themselves useful salad crops. Salad crops should be picked in the cool of the morning before the dew has left them and kept in the fridge until required so as to retain most succulent crispness; they are rarely good if gathered in the heat of the afternoon. Water well at least a day before picking! Few salads are processed, though some leaf crops can be used as spinach and frozen similarly.

Vegetables and tenderer delights

Vegetables vary hugely as to when they should be gathered. Some, such as peas, need to be watched and sampled daily to catch them in their prime, while others can be taken any time that is more convenient. If they are to be stored, roots should not be washed as this can make them less durable, though it's okay to rub off excess soil. If any have leaves that need removing, generally twist rather than cut them off, as this will reduce bleeding, and dip the damaged bits in wood ashes or sulphur dust to stop rot. Some, such as asparagus and globe artichokes, need gathering when relatively young and tender, and early in the day as with saladings, whereas main-crop potatoes may be dug any day or time when conditions permit – preferably on a dry day. As stated above, the majority of veg for processing are best picked when they are smaller and under-mature, their flesh condition being important. For storage, their skin condition is as important as their age and maturity, and it may well be better to get them in a tad early before any damage occurs than to wait and lose them.

Tender crops, such as tomatoes and peppers, are home-grown delights, but of course MUST be gathered before any frost touches them or they are likely to be ruined. As they are also relatively delicate (don't forget they are really fruits), they also require more care than the tougher crops, such as roots. This means they need a light touch and no rough handling. Indeed almost everything will be safer if baskets, trays and so on are lined with shredded paper, leaves or other soft porous padding. I grow horseradish for their big leaves to line trugs and containers for fruit.

GARDEN AND KITCHEN ESSENTIALS

Sometimes you can get by without special equipment. But it helps to have some basic tools if you are going to do a lot. Some crops are picked; others are dug. Both need careful handling – but the picked the most. Pick with your fingers and hand, not your fingertips, where possible, to spread the pressure and prevent bruising. Use a sharp knife, scissors or secateurs to cut stalks rather than force or tear at things.

Place, don't drop, items into a padded container, and never pile them up too deeply. Keep a set of clean, padded buckets, trugs, baskets and so on, specifically to pick into. Shoulder-slung bags help where you need to hang on. Soft fruit can go straight into freezer bags to save double handling; temporarily fitting the bag in a container makes it more handleable. If the fruit is falling – as with, say, blackcurrants – then put a sheet down first before picking! This is mandatory with mulberries. Old sheets or nets are also handy for nuts, as these fall for days and once on the ground are harder to spot.

For the out-of-reach there are various fruit-pickers, each essentially a long pole with a cutting ring on the end, with a collecting bag; they work, but slowly, and it may be better to invest in a good set of steps and do some effective pruning to lower the future

RIGHT ...Well a tidy desk is a sign of idle time...

crops within reach. Indeed good steps are essential – a pair and some strong planks even more effective. Never work on steps alone; always have a friend with you for safety, and to hand up and down to.

As you may really appreciate it, do try to take a kneeling pad when you go to pick low-growing stuff, and, if possible, work with your back to the wind. Unless your hair can be tied like mine, it is a good idea to wear a hat or a hairnet when you're picking fruit bushes, especially raspberries where you have to dive inside. A pair of glasses may not be necessary but may protect your eyes. When you're picking from the soil, a pair of thin gloves may make life more comfortable, and an old stiff yard brush head screwed to a post is very useful for cleaning off loose soil.

For dug crops, a fork is less likely to damage than a spade! Special forks with knobs on are made, but these are for shifting, not digging, so are of little use. A wide-spaced four-tine digging fork is needed – and do remember to push in far away, push down under and lever up. A two-tined fork does less damage in tight rows and for getting underneath prize specimens. (You can make one by cutting off the two outer extremes of a four-tined fork.) A blunt trowel may do less damage than a sharp one, and old wooden tools are finest of all for this sort of work.

Dig when the soil is drying, if you can. I place the roots in a big sieve, so leaving much of the soil behind, or onto sacks to dry a bit in the sun – never onto the ground just to have to be picked up again! Although most root crops store best unwashed, it is a good idea to have an old chip basket or small sieve and a water butt so you can wash the soil off items going straight to the kitchen. This saves soil for the garden and saves blocking drains.

A garden barrow, with an old carpet or padding cut to line it, is handy for moving trays and boxes about, but bumps them about more than if they are carried. A shed is also useful for the short-term storage of fresh items, for things being part-dried and for housing seed and fruit stores – as well as for keeping the baskets and trugs, steps, pickers and so on out of the greenhouse. The specific ways to make fruit and root stores are dealt with, along with the details of different storage methods, in the next chapter.

But that is for garden storage; for kitchen storage you would appreciate an old-fashioned pantry, facing north, cool and neither very dry nor damp. In lieu of this, we must use our kitchen shelves

RIGHT A few tools – a good trowel, 2 prong fork for lifting carrots, dibber for making holes, tamper for tamping down compost in pots, wind up/solar radio, plus a brush for hand pollination and a tin/can bottle opener for emergencies.

and cupboards; remember that everything goes off more quickly the warmer and lighter it is, so choose high – but cool – dark, dry places for dried stores, and the lower and coolest places for jammed and pickled goods. Keep long-term storage items in drawers and cupboards, where the temperature varies less than out in the room. For most things, air or damp creeping in through poor seals is fatal; you need good jars, bottles, tins or even plastic containers, all with well-fitting lids.

In the kitchen, it's worth investing in some good processing equipment – not necessarily expensive, but definitely easy to clean. There is no substitute for a good knife, a chopping board and a simple peeler; do find ones that suit you. I'm surprised how few people use peelers, which can waste far less than a knife and rarely cut you; if you've never tried, then do get one. Some funnels, sieves, drying trays and baking trays, preferably in stainless steel, are all useful in a range of sizes, though substitutes can be found. A selection of jelly bags (fine-cloth sieves) to get the finest purity is handy, as is a fruit press (see page 66). Once you start, though, you discover there are some handy gadgets such as bean slicers, pea podders and a plethora of choppers/shredders/mincers and so on, all designed to speed things up. Mechanical and electric potato or root rumblers abrade off the skin with a sandpaper drum – really handy if you like chips or prepare loads of roots. And juicers come in many forms (see page 50).

Although cookers, ranges and ovens are often not of your own choosing, the preferred option for the committed preserver has to be the old-fashioned range. Running much of the time, a good one provides perfect drying conditions above it, with ovens and hot plates for other cooking and drying processes simultaneously. Stoves with plate-heating racks or ovens are excellent. Both electric and gas ovens tend to go to searing heat when their thermostats kick in, and may not be safe – or even work – if left open as a range oven may be; however, accurate fan-assisted electric ovens left open and gas ovens can dry well. A modern gas hob is the more controllable, but for slow, untended, burn-free simmering, a range with a good ground top and ground bottom pans is hard to beat. For heating lots of pots and supplying hot water, a range may work out cheap, and although generally expensive to buy and run, it also heats the house and the hot water, dries your clothes and your boots and cheers up the kitchen – and I love to lean back against mine.

TOP Cleanliness is next to godliness. Best to clean before processing, not before storing.
BOTTOM A few good tools in the kitchen and you can do most things.

Storing and preserving

Storing and preserving

Choosing which storage method to employ can seem bewildering, but it depends on what you have, what you want and what you are prepared to do. It is most nutritious to have as much as possible nearly fresh if not absolutely fresh-picked, so simple storage should be the preferred option. But, again, it is worth storing only the near-perfect; the rest must be used, processed or lost.

The various preserving methods are applicable in varying degrees to different crops; and, of course, all is dependent on your taste – it's not much use pickling loads if you don't like vinegary things – and on your ability to follow instructions and be hygienic: processing food is a risky business, and food poisoning can kill, so be careful!

STORING IN THE GROUND AND STORES

Storage where grown: in the ground or in containers

Only a few crops are left in the ground till required, and often then some are better taken up and stored under cover in case the soil conditions preclude work outdoors. It is said that parsnips and Brussels sprouts benefit from a touch of frost, making them sweeter, so these are usually left where they've been growing. However, caution suggests that some parsnips may be better dug up in case the soil freezes solid, and laid aside under a sprinkling of soil, just in case. Sprouts may need coarse netting to keep off wood pigeons and hungry rabbits in severe weather; the same need applies to kales, Savoy cabbages and winter broccolis left to stand out all winter. Leeks are rarely bothered by much and even grow during the winter if the weather is mild enough, although again prudence suggests some should be dug, trimmed and laid aside when very cold weather threatens. Crops such as carrots, beets, chards, turnips and cabbages can be left in the ground, protected against hard frost and heavy rain either with cloches or fleeces, or under straw or shredded newspaper and plastic sheets. Covers like these work well and the crops stay in very good condition – although in warm winters they might sprout earlier than desired. The warm, protected conditions under such covers may encourage mice, slugs and other pests, so traps need to be set and regularly policed.

One of the other possibilities is growing crops in containers and moving these to a more protected place. This works well enough for some herbs and salads, not so well for others. Generally house conditions on windowsills and in conservatories are too hot and dry and yet not bright enough, so most plants get drawn, thin and soft. The hardier perennial herbs such as rosemary, thyme, sage and lavender are definitely unhappier indoors than out, though in very hard weather they may need some temporary protection. They do best on a sheltered patio, in an unheated greenhouse, or in a ventilated cold frame just to keep the worst cold off. Some salads and herbs – not the most tender sorts, of course – stay usable for months in pots if only the mud, wind and harsh weather are kept off them. And once grown many root crops, including tender ones such as sweet potatoes, store best undisturbed in the pots they've grown in. Without doubt moving plants under cool cover also usefully extends the season of fruits such as grapes, citrus and redcurrants, which are then retained fresher on their bush for longer than if picked. And then of course there's the ingenious orchard-house method of bringing plants in under unheated cover from the end of winter to encourage earlier crops.

PAGES 26–27 **A comfortable shed for drying and storing is handy.**
BELOW **When winter comes you need a full store – though there is always something to be found in the garden.**
OPPOSITE **Leeks can be grown in tubs where water is handy and be brought under cover when frosts stop outdoor crops being dug.**

Storing in root, fruit, seed and herb stores

As mentioned earlier, there is little point taking the effort to pick and store anything that's less than perfect, as it will surely rot before you come to use it. So select ruthlessly, send the imperfect off to process in some way, leaving only the very good to pack away – and then police these as well. Inspect regularly and dispose of any rots before they spread. And be ever vigilant of rodents, slugs and other pests nibbling away at your treasures; set traps before they cause damage.

Root cellars were once commonplace. Modern cellars are likely to be too dry and warm; an old disused backyard air-raid shelter would make a good root cellar – dark, cold, but not likely to freeze, damp but not running with water, and with not quite stagnant air. A dead fridge or freezer unit or two in a shaded shed can provide a simple alternative. Such units are well insulated, rodent-proof and dark, and have a constant temperature. They're also airtight, so you need to make holes in the seal to allow some airflow – note that these holes should not be big enough to admit mice. Likewise a small shed, cloche or cold frame in a shady spot can, with lots of extra insulation, be converted into a passably good store.

Another alternative is to sink a couple of plastic dustbins in a shady spot – making sure they won't be flooded – and then make an insulated cover or quilt for each from plastic bags, newspaper, or whatever to keep off the worst of the chills from above. Unless you fit a small chimney, with an anti-rain device, these do not breathe, so very damp stores may be more inclined to moulder – and a false floor may be needed to prevent the lowest layer from standing in condensed water. But even without a chimney, they work well for crops packed away in good condition, and are especially handy for dried crops in well-sealed rustproof containers.

Most roots keep best when kept cool in slightly moist air that changes slowly. Traditionally, huge clamps were made of long piles covered in layers of straw, soil, then straw again, and topped with thatch. Of course, these were for feeding livestock as much as people – carrots are good food for either – so enormous clamps were necessary. You can do a similar thing with modern materials: pack carrots and other roots in mounds – or preferably in boxes of ever so slightly moist sand – and cover them with masses of straw, then old carpet or blankets or newspapers, then a plastic sheet or three. This will keep out all but arctic weather. But for smaller and diverse household quantities, a dead fridge or freezer in a shed or garage is handier. Roots packed in bags of peat or sand obviously fare much better than those loose in bags or nets, which are more likely to wither and rot in less than perfect conditions. Never leave

roots or fruits or much else to sit where strong smells abound; at least drop them in a plastic bag or dustbin.

What you can store

Carrots, beets, celery and celeriac, Spanish and winter radish, salsify, turnips and swedes all store well. Kohl-rabi is a very good long keeper and rivals hard white cabbage. Other roots, such as those of Jerusalem artichokes, Chinese artichokes, scorzonera and chicory, are harder to dig and store without damage and are often better left in situ and protected. (Chicory may, of course, be dug and packed in moist sand in boxes and forced in the dark and warm to give chicon sprouts for salad.)

The best roots can be individually packed in layers of slightly moist sand, peat or whatever, preferably in self-stacking boxes. Second-grade roots are best unwashed and packed carefully in trays or boxes: use plastic or treated metal, as the damp will rot wood or cardboard. Any amounts can be easily packed in plastic netting sacks, but these give less protection from damage.

At a push, cabbages, cauliflowers, sprouts, leeks and other non-root crops can be kept along with roots; cross-taint may occur but is not too damaging. Potatoes, though, really deserve a separate store as they pick up taints too easily, and they need somewhere less cold as, if they get even close to freezing, they go sweet (whereas most other roots are fine if they're not actually frozen). A separate potato store is also a good idea because in really cold periods extra warmth can be provided to the spuds – for example with hot-water bottles – and then, in spring, their usable length in store can be increased if you prevent withering and sprouting by cooling them – likewise with frozen-water bottles put in to defrost. Potatoes must be kept in the dark or they go green and become poisonous! Do not transfer them to the kitchen 'tray' until required. It makes a lot of sense to put mousetraps and slug pubs (saucers of beer) in amongst your stored root crops – preferably where cats can't get at them!

TOP LEFT **They may look better, but don't wash things you are going to store for long as they keep better dirty.**
BOTTOM LEFT **Potatoes in a dead freezer root store keep firm as it is slightly damp but need be in plastic trays or boxes – paper bags collapse.**
RIGHT **A dead refrigerator makes an excellent fruit store – insulated and rodent-proof – some even have a lock!**

Fruit stores are similar, except that they need more airflow than root stores. Indeed, the best are very airy – but then the fruit withers rather quickly; while the more stagnant suffer the danger of one ripe variety's causing all the others to ripen too soon. Once again, redundant fridge and freezer units or similar well-insulated rodent-proof containers are alternatives, again housed in a shady shed or similar. Old bookshelves and chests of drawers can be pressed into service; fruit is more precious than the roots relegated to sacks on the floor. The aim is to keep the fruit – usually predominantly apples – in good condition for as long as possible. This means separating early keepers from late keepers, and using each variety in turn so you remove any ripening ones before they bring on the others. USE LABELS! Any of the real earlies should never go near the store but be processed; they rarely last more than a month at best, anyway.

Apples

It needs saying again that apples can keep only if perfect and with their pedicel – little stalk – intact. The best, those you want to give to friends or use for a special occasion (and that you know will keep till that date), can be individually wrapped; I use newspaper

– kitchen towel might be better – and then pack them carefully in their own box or tray and label them. The longest keepers can also be wrapped; some people oil the paper first – sunflower oil would be the least intrusive. You can also lay apples on a bed of shredded paper; adding more as padding before another layer works well.

Dry leaves have been used, but this method risks pests and taint. Likewise, hay is susceptible to moulds and taints; straw is better – and dried stinging nettles are thought good by some. Old books claim that all fruits, first ever so slightly dried, can be packed in dry sand and will keep for many months longer than usual. Others swear by simply packing apples into plastic bags and pricking these with the odd hole before storing them away. A large number of my apples stored for later juicing are packed, gently, in buckets which I just stand in a shed. Most of all storability is about suitable varieties grown well and gently handled, and being kept safe from decay and rodents.

Pears

Pears should not be mixed with apples. Not only do they cross-taint, but they need different conditions – pears liking it warmer and more humid than apples (and no pears worth having last very long). For most people the best place both to store and to ripen pears – which for most varieties is the same thing – is under the bed, or possibly in a cool corner of the kitchen. There, they can get the twice-daily inspection pears need, and be brought out to the table as soon as they colour up. They bruise even more easily than apples, and the best need to be laid on and separated by soft shredded paper in trays. That said, I do house a lot of my longest-keeping pears in several layers of sawdust or leaves in buckets stood in a rodent-proof cupboard.

Other fruit and veg

Grapes on the stem in bottles of water are best stood somewhere with more ventilation than a small fruit store, as they need sufficient airflow to prevent them from going musty – but not so much as to dry them out. (The Victorians reckoned they kept longest and best in a warm, sealed room on their own – but I doubt it.) A frost-free spare room or rodent-free garage is about perfect. If you have a less secure store, keep them in a recycled birdcage, otherwise they are sure to be stolen by small birds, if not rodents.

A hanging safe box is an excellent thing to have anyway – a secure place for other things such as fresh fruit, meat, cheese and so on. The principle is of a lightweight cupboard of wood framing set with panels of perforated zinc (modern ones tend to be plastic

and not as durable). The whole thing is then suspended on wires or stood on unclimbable supports in a cool shady shed. The top is made solid and with extended eaves to keep out dust, and to prevent certain flies from dropping their eggs through – or even live young! This is a good place to put such valuable but enticing stores as grapes, or to use for dried goods. It also serves well for storing the short-lived fruits such as figs, and the pongy such as quinces. And it's a good place to store nuts.

In all stores it pays to have not only mousetraps and rat bait but also, perhaps surprisingly, cockroach traps, as these are becoming more of a pest, and slug traps. Slugs are attracted to fruit and may romp in the comparative warmth of your store doing untold damage. One friend, when given this tip for potatoes, 'Put slug pubs in about the spuds and the slugs will drown themselves, thus stopping further damage,' pronounced that he'd do it in his apple store too, as slugs were ruining them – which provoked laughter from everyone, as it confirmed our suspicions that he never picked till too late when they were all windfalls and full of slugs anyway.

A shed or garage with a cool dry roof space is ideal for onions, garlic and shallots, which keep best slung in shallow nets. But this definitely shouldn't be the same place as where you store grapes, as these would pick up their smell! Many used to hang their onions under eaves or, better, inside the roofs of their woodsheds where they were cool and dry and would not taint. The various long-keeping squashes like to be kept in a warmer (but not hot) dry room, and preferably slung in nets or laid in trays on shredded newspaper. Try keeping them in a warm spare room – or hide them behind your sofa!

ABOVE **Not the living room, honest!**
OPPOSITE PAGE **This bit, the stalk/pedicel is crucial; without it the fruit will not keep long.**

DRYING

Drying is one of the oldest ways of preserving foods, as it happens naturally. Fruits may dry while still attached to the tree or vine: the pulp dries, though not the seeds, and remains edible as long as it doesn't go mouldy first. Seeds desiccate themselves before spreading, reducing their moisture content so that they can lie dormant. And, conveniently, while leaves and flowers cut off in their prime do wither and fade, they may, nevertheless, retain much of their original colour, form and scent far longer than if left on the plant.

Traditionally, whole civilisations have relied on the long-term storage of dried crops, especially grains such as wheat, rice and maize, not only as a mainstay but to bridge the years of shortages and famines. A number of storage methods were possible but, for

LEFT **It's amazing how much the stuff shrinks when it's dried.**

OPPOSITE TOP **As uniform as possible, or some bits shrivel and others stay soft, and you wouldn't want that.**

OPPOSITE BOTTOM **Spacing them uniformly on a clean cane is simpler than on string.**

endurance little beat using sealed pots of dry grain buried some-where safe. Throughout history most of our livestock in temperate climates have been fed on hay and other dried fodder throughout half the year. (Tree twigs and leaves of hazel, lime and elm used to be grown and dried for animal feed, as well as the usual grass and herbage hays.)

It is said that drying foods retains more of their natural goodness longer than other methods of preservation. Sadly, though, however well the drying and rehydration is done there are few foods that are improved by the process. Perhaps some of the pulses come close. However, the dried food may become a choice item in itself – such as raisins, from grapes – which may even be

better than the original. I would certainly claim that dried Asian pear rings are a far more enjoyable treat than the fresh fruit.

Drying food as a means of preservation relies on the low moisture content, preventing moulds and decay. This has often been combined with the protection of salting and/or smoking, especially for meat products. But drying can be sufficient on its own, as long as the food remains completely dry and, in most cases, sealed in the cool and dark. The percentage concentration of sugars, minerals and salts in foods increases as the water is removed – and this is significant for many fruits: their sweetness and acidity may be so greatly enhanced during their preservation that they will keep while still quite moist – far moister than the level tolerated by vegetables or other foodstuffs. Fruits such as prunes, raisins, figs and so on, all keep while considerably moister than seeds, herbs or dried vegetables. So, unless you are good at sealing their containers, these different groups should never be kept in the same drawer or cupboard. It is always safest to keep dried food in dry places: the smallest leak and a hint of damp will get to it.

Dried foods are useful in the pantry, as they can endure so well and are always there if needed – though, for most purposes, they are best when you can plan ahead, as they may need time to rehydrate, soak or sprout. This can be an opportunity to add extra flavour, for example by soaking your pulses overnight with herb-, honey- or wine-flavoured water in the same way as you would use a marinade. Be careful not to make your soaking liquid too strong, too sweet or too salty, as this will make pulses hard and slow the rehydration of other things. In other words, a little brandy, wine or honey in the water will flavour apple rings as you soak them, while too much may turn them into another preserve entirely.

For drying, as for other methods, prime produce in tiptop condition is the only sort worth considering. This is all the more so where a lot of effort has to be made, though, of course, things like dried peas and beans can be had by just collecting the haulm and pods. For the drying of fresh fruits and vegetables there must be a source of dry air – usually warm because that makes it effectively drier. (But cold, dry air can work too: commercial freeze-drying chills the air to take out all its water so that it sucks the water out of food faster and without warming it up.)

You can buy food-dryers, make your own, use a warm but not hot oven in an old-fashioned range, or use a ventilated airing cupboard – or a solar-heated one in sunnier climes. Or just hang the items on string suspended somewhere with dry air passing through. For smaller items you may prefer wire trays to stringing

up. The detail is not important: all you need is dry air passing over the food. Although warm is okay, too warm can be a problem because the item may cook or even caramelise! What is needed is a sufficient flow of dry air to dry the surfaces before they start to go mouldy.

Once the surfaces have 'healed over', the insides can dry out more slowly. So it pays to space items well and ensure their conditions are good at the start; once they are partly dried they can be repositioned much closer together to be finished off. Unless your dryer or system is very expensive, some spots will undoubtedly prove hotter or drier than others; too hot too soon makes for hard crusts with soggy insides. For a more uniform product, move your items about, giving each a 'go' in a good spot – though, of course, this involves more labour. It is possible, once the initial surface is dry, to continue the drying intermittently over a longer period using the fading warmth of a domestic oven after cooking.

Needless to say, peeling is needed for thick-skinned subjects, and some fruits may need stoning to save space and prevent taint. The thinner you cut any slices or pieces, the quicker they dry. However, if they're too thin they may cook or go crispy, flake or crumble too easily. The odd extra thick piece here and there may leave the middle still damp when everything seems dry, and later in storage that moisture may redistribute and moulder the lot. Thus it is best to strive for uniformly sized pieces, at least with no very thick bits. With herbs, take care with their stalks.

Fruit pieces can be coated in sugar or sugar solution before drying to give them added protection and prevent browning, but this usually makes them stickier. Salt or salty water can be used similarly with vegetables, although this may cause problems later as you'll need to reduce or remove the salt unless a very salty product is desired. Culinary starch, corn or even wheat flour can also be used to seal sticky surfaces with an innocuous coating which discourages some pests and makes handling easier. And, of course, dust and flies must always be totally excluded, most especially at the beginning when the surfaces are wet.

Once the materials are dried as well as you can achieve, this may still not be enough and they might need finishing off in a gentle oven with the door open. Then they will need to be packed away where the light and damp air can't get at them. The less they are handled the better. And do make sure your containers are airtight, rodent-proof and well labelled. You may or may not wish to eat the contents when they get very old, but it might be nice to know what they were and when they were laid down if you think you may ever have to!

Fruit

Among the fruits, apple rings are easy to dry, but they're a bit pappy – and as ordinary storage keeps apples available for more than half the year anyway, they're not really a high priority. But they can be useful, either reconstituted or more likely as snacks. Pears can be a tad 'greasy' when dried, but they're more useful than apples as their season is shorter; instead of making rings, I peel, halve and de-core them, as this is less wasteful. I've never dried quinces, but I guess with a good power saw you could try slicing them. Plums, whatever their colour, all seem to turn into the blackish purple variety of prunes whatever I try – some very nice prunes, but always the same. The Asian or Nashi pear is superb eating only when it's dried, when it loses its fresh grittiness and odd perfume and becomes a chewy gourmet treat rivalling the finest raisins. Apricots and peaches dry to prune-like forms unless you are careful – but these are more tasty than plum-derived prunes by far! Grapes are just a must, as having your own raisins and sultanas is such a delight. Other small fruits are a bit fiddly, lose their colour, and are seedy and prone to mould early on, but are quite possible.

Herbs

Herbs are generally easy to dry, although some are barely worth the effort. Dried mint and dried basil are poor compared with fresh, or with the leaves preserved by other methods. Bay, on the other hand, seems to get better the longer it has been dried. Most other herbs can be dried easily and successfully. And as so little is needed at a time, it makes sense to grow a big batch of any given herb one year and to dry enough of it to keep you going over the next few. It is said that herbs are best gathered in early morning, as soon as the dew has dried off them. They are generally easy to dry: just hanging them over a string in a cool, airy, shady place is remarkably effective. Tying them in bunches risks mouldy middles; tying each stalk separately is tedious; sometimes you can hook them over the string by a side-shoot, but then they may slide together if the string is not taut. A simple solution: invest in a pile of wooden clothes pegs and use these to grip the stalks in place. (If you are really methodical, the pegs could be permanently threaded on and fixed at mathematically regular intervals.) Once fully dried, do not leave herbs to lose their flavour but seal them in paper bags in containers.

Mixed herbs

Although most of the time we keep our various dried herbs separate, it is quite possible to make up mixtures instead. I often collect a wide range of various herbs and salad leaves (see Flowerdew's super salad, page 129) to eat with my meals. I tried taking a portion and simply drying it out – after all, it made a palatable blend of flavours fresh. And so it did when dried: crumbled and sieved it made a unique condiment to be mixed into salads with mayonnaise or a dressing to moisten the blend before eating. I suppose you could dry almost any salad leaves, including lettuce, and store them for winter use – though I've not noted many people trying it.

For winter use, I do collect posies of mixed herbs, particularly rosemary and sage with hyssop and lavender, for making up teas, tisanes and infusions. You can make coarser and bigger mixed-herb posies for inserting in a stocking and hanging in the bath; these might especially feature lavender, with rosemary, sage and thyme, but also perhaps camomile, lemon verbena and mint – though too much of the last may mean you get a green bath.

Once carefully dried, herbs need to be picked and sieved to remove stalks, detritus and dust, and then packed in paper bags in dark jars or tins and stored in dry, cool and dark conditions. It is said that even tightly sealed containers are no good for dried herbs if there's any surrounding damp at all, as if the containers breathe ever so slightly the damp gets in – and even if they don't breathe, the inside can go musty anyway. So, ideally, most herbs should be stored in paper bags or well-sealed dark jars in a cool dry place – that means another dead fridge, I'm afraid, or the seed store. If the herbs are of the coarser varieties, or more for show than for consumption, they can be left to hang in bunches from a dry ceiling.

Vegetables

Vegetables can be dried with little trouble and are then very handy for soups, stews and garnishes. Onion rings are obvious for stringing (the unusable little centres can be pickled or chutneyed), as are carrots, which are most easily strung as longitudinal slices with a needle on thread. I haven't tried drying many other roots, though,

OPPPOSITE PAGE Herbs can be pegged on a string a lot quicker than tying and more surely than just hooking a bit over.
ABOVE Peel and slice, then separate into the bits which can be used for curry bases, sauces and so on, and hang the whole large rings, which are worth drying on a cane – and simpler than this string (for the photographer you understand!), which they slip on.

as they keep so well anyway. Both French green beans and green runner beans can be dried if thinly sliced and blanched first. Tomatoes and sweet peppers will dry easily, since they are really fruits. The firmer-fleshed Italian plum tomatoes and special varieties are easier to dry than the juicier ones we normally grow in the UK. Hot (chilli) peppers are so easy to dry they are a must; sweet peppers are also worth a go – their high vitamin value makes them a good addition to winter soups and stews – although, to be fair, they are more convenient frozen. Most other salads and vegetables, for example courgettes and cabbages, are technically possible to dry, but to questionable advantage. More importantly, many vegetable crops are actually seeds – a unique range of special dried foods in their own right.

SEED AND NUT CROPS

These are nature's gift: foods that preserve themselves naturally with little effort, are packed full of fats, minerals and proteins, and keep for a long time. Their only drawbacks are that rodents love them most of all, and that many need time for reconstituting with water; they're not instant like most other natural products. Almost all dried products benefit from, or actually need, soaking at least overnight to get palatable results. Yet, while many dried products do not much resemble the original when rehydrated, seeds are indeed reborn. And, of course, if kept well and still viable, they may be sprouted instead of soaked and cooked. It is said that Pharaoh's pea and several others were found in, as you may imagine, a pyramid. While this claim may be dubious, seeds do have incredible longevity, and keep their vital powers and food value intact for decades, even centuries. This is precisely why they are so useful: they are designed to dry and to keep. Seeds such as wheat, barley, rye and oats are probably a bit adventurous for the average garden plot, but sweet corn, sunflowers and pumpkin seeds are dead easy, as are the most useful: pulses, peas and beans.

Although special sorts of peas and beans are grown for drying, almost any that are grown for the green pod or seed will dry almost as well; it's just that the size, texture or flavour will not be as good. Generally peas, even the sorts grown for drying, are less useful after drying than beans. Drying most pulses could not be simpler: once the haulm and pods have dried, but before they split and shed, you gather them up. They keep well in their pods attached to the haulm, hung in a dry, airy roof space; you can hang them up in nylon net curtains to catch any that drop. Unfortunately, pulses are

prone to rodent and bird theft, so are much safer once fully dried, podded, sifted and sorted and packed in tins or jars.

Other seed crops – sunflowers especially – suffer as much from rodent and bird theft while still in the plot, so may need protecting with net bags or similar. Pumpkin seeds are a nutritious treat and easily dried. Crops of seeds such as poppy, nigella, celery, mustard, caraway and so on may need their seed heads tying into paper bags to catch the crop before it disperses. Most can be cut after flowering and before the seeds have dispersed, the whole top of the plant left to dry on paper sheets in a dry place and turned regularly until the seeds can be threshed out. If the tops are hung up they may drop their seeds, so need bags hanging around them – more clothes pegs. The seeds, once cleaned, can be stored in paper bags in jars or tins.

Nuts are best eaten fresh, but if well dried in their shells they can be packed in dry salt in boxes and then, if kept somewhere cool and dry, can retain their value for many years in the case of hazelnuts – less for others. When fresh, they need to be kept well aired; the best solution is nets or bags, preferably of wire, hung in dry roof spaces or on greenhouse staging – even better if these are also rodent- and squirrel-proof. Nuts can be salted and smoked to give them good flavour, but then need to be eaten promptly as they may go rancid.

Specific seed and nut stores are not essential but useful; they need to be cool and very dry, as well as completely rodent-proof. And, as seeds and nuts may be stored for longer than a year, you need to be extra careful of their theft not only by birds and squirrels but also by small bugs and even ants. A good wooden box with a tight lid may do for the garden seeds, but will not hold enough quantity for food storage. A metal one is more secure than wood, but varies too much in temperature unless well positioned. Not surprisingly, perhaps, once again a dead fridge is perfect, especially if it's also equipped with some silica-gel bags to mop up any humidity. Rodent-proof, compact and stood in a cool dry shed, it will provide near constant conditions.

OPPOSITE PAGE When picking nuts pick them all – do not waste time selecting only the good as if you leave the bad you will re-examine them next collection.
THIS PAGE (left to right) Select out the good nuts for use or store and compost the rest or use them for smoking food. Poppy seed has to be gathered before the heads open and have their seed shaken out. Beans can be kept in the pod on the dried haulm – if mice can't reach them.

SOAKING AND SPROUTING

Although some dried products are used as they come – nuts, raisins and dried fruits – the majority, especially the seeds, need soaking for some time before they can be used. (Finely divided herbs, and powdered or finely chopped fruits and vegetables, can be added to many dishes, but risk turning chewy or gritty if fried or roasted without first absorbing some added moisture.) Obviously, the smaller the item the quicker it will rehydrate, so onion rings and sweet-pepper pieces take less time than, say, prunes. Hot water may harden items and warm water may encourage mould, so use cold water and leave the soaking items in a covered container in the fridge or another cool place. Overnight is usually the minimum! Over a day's soaking may be required; then bring the items to boil in the water they have soaked in.

Although you can add flavourings to the water – anything from brandy or honey to herbs, garlic, salt and pepper – be careful not to make the solution strong or it will not soak in properly. This is especially true for pulses, peas and beans, which will cook hard if you salt their soaking water. (And most pulses need at least twenty minutes at a rolling boil to ensure they are safe to eat – especially red kidney beans.) You can usually add any surplus soaking and boiling water to the dish, although with salted dried vegetables you may have to discard some or it could overwhelm.

The water from sprouting seeds is not so palatable. It needs to be replaced every six hours with fresh, and is best thrown onto the compost heap as it's full of by-products from the seeds – which can mould them if it's not replaced. Sprouting seeds is a very good way of getting more for less. The nutritional value is much better and the bulk and texture can greatly improve. When sprouting, the well-washed seeds should be soaked in surplus warm water, preferably well aerated (shake it vigorously in a half-empty bottle), rinsed and changed regularly and kept in the warm and dark, say in an airing cupboard. Once they have sprouted, they can be moved to the fridge to slow down further growth; very few types should be shown the light as this makes them green and bitter.

A good DIY sprouter is a largish brown glass jar with a wide plastic lid. Carefully make many small holes in the lid; allowing the seeds to breathe and acting as the sieve when you're draining the water with each change. Put only a few spoonfuls of seeds in the bottom – they expand manyfold as they absorb water. Most are best when the seed leaves have expanded but before the real ones are formed; only some, such as rocket, remain edible and tasty as they get bigger. Almost all seeds of the crops with leaves we eat have edible sprouts (if they're cooked), but the seedlings of plants with fruits or roots we eat may be inedible or even poisonous. You

should not eat sprouted tomato or potato seedlings, for example. Pulses need careful cooking once sprouted anyway; not all are edible. I've never heard of anyone sprouting runner-bean seed to eat – and, as the roots are poisonous, it's probably a good job.

LEATHERING

This is a little-known form of drying more akin to jam-making. A much neglected art, it offers a way of converting almost every fruit surplus into a very attractive long-storing product. It's very simple: you take a plentiful fruit, such as apples or pears, which you wash and chop and simmer down to a pulp – skins, pips, stalks and all – along with roughly a quarter of the amount of a flavouring fruit, say blackcurrants, plums or raspberries. Subtler fruits, such as strawberries, are best mixed with unripe or cooking apples to get more bite, while acid fruits, such as redcurrants, go better with sweet dessert apples. If the fruits are very dry, like blackcurrants, I add some apple juice to help the initial breakdown. Once your mixed fruits have all broken down to a paste over a slow heat, sieve out the roughage and reduce the purée to a thick paste by further slow simmering. Pour about a finger thickness of this onto well-greased trays and dry in an airy warm place or open oven. The paste soon turns to a sheet of leather-like material which can be peeled off the tray, hung and dried further. It truly resembles leather and you could make a hat out of it.

The drying so concentrates the flavour and acidity that no extra sugar is required. To reduce stickiness, rub fine sugar onto the surface – or cornstarch works better, used in moderation. Leather can be reconstituted to make a fruity paste for all sorts of uses, but is best eaten just as it is, cut into long strings or small shapes as natural chews. The softer forms need to be stored more carefully than those dried rigid. Fruit leather can make unusual bases for cheesecakes, create fruit lasagnes and appear in trifles or cut into decorative chewy garnishes. A sheet of apricot/strawberry and apple leather is the basis of my celebrated rum-butter Swiss roll. Of course, the idea is to store it, not eat it all right away. Packed in a sealed jar, it will keep for years, slowly becoming more vinously flavourful. The meat equivalent is pemmican or jerky. It is possible a vegetable leather could be made with, say, carrot as the base – but as this would probably go mouldy rather quickly it might need smoking to help preserve it.

OPPOSITE PAGE **Dried beans need soaking for some time before flavourings can be added, and only in moderation or they will cook hard.**
THIS PAGE **Make a really thick purée of almost any fruits, sieving out the skins and seeds, then pour a thick layer in a wide greased tin and dry slowly, and you get a chewy, delicious and healthy sweet (the sugar coating is just to soak up some stickiness).**

SMOKING, HOT AND COLD

Smoked foods are now a contentious issue. Without doubt, some of the substances found in smoke are bad for us – but then so are some foods, and indeed life itself. How much pollution do you ingest from a couple of smoked rashers compared with that from a short walk next to a busy city road? Anyway, I prefer the taste of the former.

Although smoking is mostly considered a flavouring and preserving method for meats and cheeses, it's quite common to smoke other foods: smoked paprika is much used (indeed a cunning addition as a garnish, and included in most of my savoury dishes – try it and see!); smoked garlic is well known and smoked eggs a delicacy. Smoked bilberries and whinberries are traditional with hunters and campers, while nuts of all kinds, often sold salted and roasted, can be smoked too, as can sunflower and pumpkin seeds. All taste good and, in some cases, smoking may help them keep longer. Why not smoked onions, carrots and potatoes? There is even a delicious smoke-enhanced wine, Pouilly-Fumé; generous and grateful readers may send me a few bottles anytime… Cheers.

Anyway, smoking is a much under-utilised way of further preserving food already protected by other means, such as drying and salting. The smoke is itself strongly antiseptic, so – quite apart from any drying by contact or prior treatment – little goes mouldy where it's been exposed to a lot of smoke. But since smoking is only a surface effect and takes time to penetrate, there's a need for other methods as well; in fact, overdoing the smoking may give a bitter taste.

Cold smoking

The flavour obtained depends on the wood burned, or rather smouldered – apple and hickory are reckoned the best – and on the temperature: most smoking is best done with really cool smoke, not hot. The time smoking takes means the food dries out and lets smoke soak into the surface; then the maturing for weeks afterwards allows the tasty aroma to permeate through.

Smoking does not need to be complicated. I smoulder fruit-wood sawdust in my wood stove and simply hang stuff down into the chimney through the pot up on the roof. Others use long pipes to cool smoke from a separate small burner, or pass the smoke through earth troughs covered in planks, and then through an old barrel containing the items to be smoked. The key is to get cool smoke. The skill is not in the construction – anything works, near enough – but in keeping a small smouldering fire going, and not letting it get too hot, for enough hours to give a good smoking.

The minimum is at least a whole morning; many items require a half-day or night or more. Then you have to be patient, because the taste of freshly smoked food is not nice – it's almost like creosote. Wrap the food, first in greaseproof paper and then in newspaper; this keeps the smoke in to mature as the flavour permeates through and becomes much pleasanter. The smoked food needs be stored in a cool dry place to mature, and not with other things that may pick up the aroma.

Zucchini bacon

My personal invention from my vegetarian days is fat zucchini bacon. Slice small marrows or huge zucchini (or courgettes) lengthwise into wide strips the thickness of your little finger, with one edge thinly peeled, but leaving the peel along the other edge as a 'rind'. Soak the slices in brine for an hour or so, then string them up to dry. Once they're dry but still malleable, take them down and brush them with oil, herbs and seasoning, pack them together, tightly string them about and smoke them; then wrap them in brown paper, then tinfoil and put to mature in the fridge. It really is nothing like bacon – but very good, anyway.

Hot smoking

Hot smoking adds a whole new depth to foods you already cook, usually restricted to the flavours produced by barbecuing, and although not a preservation method it does add so much value it's worth the mention. Any chipped wood, dampened sawdust, bunch of herbs or just small prunings added to a barbecue will, if well dampened, smoke not burn and so add a wonderful flavour – nut and fruit woods being the best. It should be done towards the end, and lightly, with good flavoured woods – and not overdone, as too much will be unpleasant and bitter, just as with cold smoking. You can cheat by using an old-fashioned bellows bee smoker filled with smouldering sticks, leaves and sawdust to finish off food cooked in an ordinary oven or under a grill. For that authentic Jamaican flavour, it's hard to beat smouldering guava leaves (I grow these just for that purpose) which finish off my jerk real fine. (Burning pimento wood or bay rum leaves would be better, but these are harder to grow.)

LEFT Smouldering fruit wood sawdust in my woodstove hot-smokes some zucchini bacon for short term storage (well not very long as it is too good).

FREEZING

Freezing has a longer history than you may imagine; keeping food chilled is not such a modern invention. And the oldest naturally frozen food is still uncovered in the Arctic: deep-frozen mammoth is apparently still edible after tens of thousands of years. Making use of the knowledge that cold preserves was hampered by the lack of means of exploiting it: Roger Bacon, the great Renaissance scientist, died catching cold while experimenting with freezing a chicken to preserve it. Ice houses from previous centuries were indeed used for storing meat and so on, but were built far more for storing ice – this to be combined with salt to get the low temperatures required to make ice creams and sorbets, newly introduced from the Italian courts. The first mechanical freezers were invented by the Victorians and soon introduced on a domestic scale for the rich, and on boats for long-term transport of perishable goods. Freezing food at home has become easier with modern units, which are totally reliable. They involve only a modest capital outlay, and a big one costs little more than a small one. A bigger freezer is so much more use and more efficient per cubic foot, and only marginally more expensive to run than a small one – so always overbuy. Of course, almost every freezer runs on electricity and this involves a carbon footprint – but so do jamming, bottling and cooking in general, anyway. And you amply offset the carbon running costs by the saving in food miles you make by preserving your own.

A deep freezer is useful in many ways, not only for long-term storage from this cropping season till next, but also for the short-term holding of a crop until it's convenient to deal with – or as a way of pre-processing. Many of my jams and syrups are made from briefly frozen fruit; once the fruit has been burst by freezing, the juice separates easily.

You don't have to go out of your way to freeze large batches, though. During the productive season, whenever you prepare meals with your own fresh produce it makes sense to make too much, and then freeze ready-to-reheat portions, either of individual fruits or vegetables, or of whole meals. For this, plastic cups are very handy; once frozen and well labelled the cups can be repacked in freezer bags. Although plastic boxes are most efficient when full and are easy to stack and move, their lids stick and are brittle, and they waste space as they become empty. Plastic bags for freezing are sloppy, hard to keep in order, and need tying or closing with a clothes peg or wire tie to prevent them swapping flavours with everything else – although obviously one big plus point is that clear bags often need no label! A combination of boxes and bags is most practical, with the bags moving inside suitable half-empty boxes. I save plastic drinks bottles, to wash and reuse for freezing juices, and wax cartons for the purées.

A way to make bags pack more economically is – before you fill them – to stand each one in a rectangular cardboard shape-former, made from the base of a cereal packet or fruit-juice box, and then fill it with the partly frozen pieces or purée or whatever. Once the shape has set solid, the cardboard box can be removed and reused for another bag.

A very sensible idea is not only to label each item – with ID and date! – but also to compile a list detailing contents and position – for example 'four bags raspberries, blue box, lower left-hand side, two bags strawberries plus half-box blackcurrants lower left-hand side, herbs all in green box upper right-hand side' – and attach it to the outside of the unit. It then makes sense to update the list as you either put in or take out items. Otherwise there is a tendency for stuff to 'go dormant' until it is past using with much comfort.

Fruit

Most fruits are easy to freeze, needing no more than to be cleaned, dried, laid on oiled trays to freeze and, once solid, popped into labelled bags or tubs to be taken piecemeal as required. Ideally, any air should be sucked or squeezed out of bags. Fruit portions can be dipped in sugared or even salted water to stop discoloration and the 'freezer burn' drying-off of their surface – make sure your trays are well oiled, though, as wet fruit is more prone to stick. Or freeze them in portion-controlled amounts that have been sugared overnight to withdraw some of their juices. Or they can be frozen fresh, packed in sugar syrup or fruit juice, their own or another. Freezing mixtures ready for use will save you time later. Turning fruits into juices, ices and sorbets saves space and can mean even more get eaten.

The stone fruits need to have their stones removed before freezing, as these taint the fruit – and eventually everything else – with a flavour of bitter almond. Most skins are easier to remove after freezing and before the fruit is thawed; simply pass each fruit under hot water and the skin can be slipped off before the inside starts to melt.

LEFT A thick coating of sugar on top of the raspberries before they go into the freezer sucks the juices out without heat.

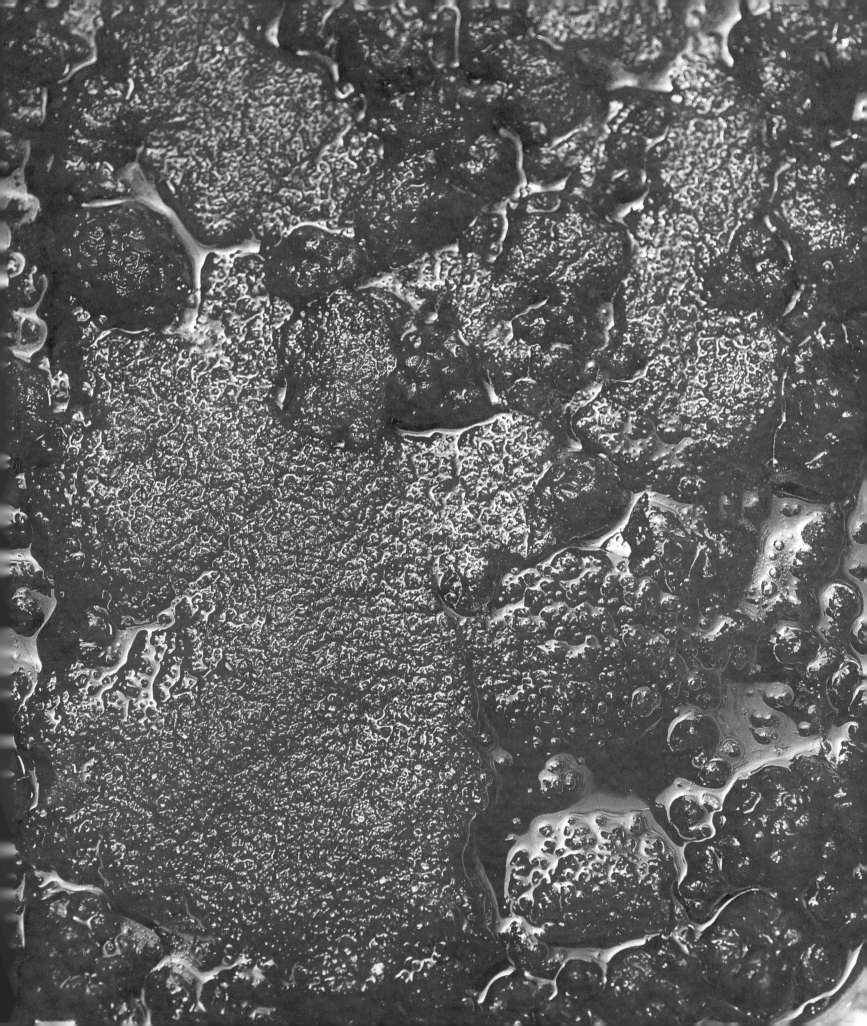

Vegetables

Vegetables require more care if they are to be frozen: first of all they need to be not only cleaned and cut into small uniform bits, but also blanched. This is to disrupt their enzymes and help preserve some of their texture. Blanching is simply heating the items to boiling point, or near enough, for from 3–5 minutes, and then immediately cooling rapidly in very cold, even icy water. After cooling, drain, gently roll on a clean dry tea towel and then freeze on well-oiled trays before repacking into bags. Most useful for this simple method I reckon are sliced green beans, peas, broad beans and then sweet corn, which can be added to almost anything. Carrots and other roots can be sliced, cut small or cubed to make them a more even size before freezing.

Tomatoes and sweet peppers are both to be treated more like fruits, and frozen as they come – the tomatoes whole and un-skinned, or skinned and chopped; the peppers cleaned and cut into small chunks. Mushrooms can be frozen, but they dry and rehydrate so readily it seems pointless for most, though I have often successfully frozen fried giant puffball steaks. The gourmet crops, such as asparagus and globe artichokes, can be blanched and frozen, but may as well be fully cooked first and then need only defrosting later. The tips and hearts are much more economical of space than the whole spears and heads! The soup and stock are even more compact, and worth considering even if you don't fancy freezing the titbits alone. With these gourmet crops it's a good idea to freeze them on oiled trays, and it's worth sealing them first under plastic film or oiled foil, to save the aroma permeating the freezer.

The problem that can arise with freezing onions and garlic, and anything containing much of them – as with other strong-smelling produce – is cross-taint. So beware and have good seals on everything. You do not get nice results freezing fresh garlic or onions – a bit unpleasant, in fact, though less so if they're blanched or fried first. Meals containing these alliums can be frozen, if well sealed, but it might be better to keep them out of stocks and bases specially made for freezing and to add them later, after thawing.

With some vegetables, a good alternative to blanching before freezing is to partially fry them first – this works well for battered onion rings and especially well for potato chips. For confirmed chip addicts like me this is the method to get real home-grown choice main-crop variety chips when the stored crop has long gone or sprouted and the new crop is still months away. Pre-frying is

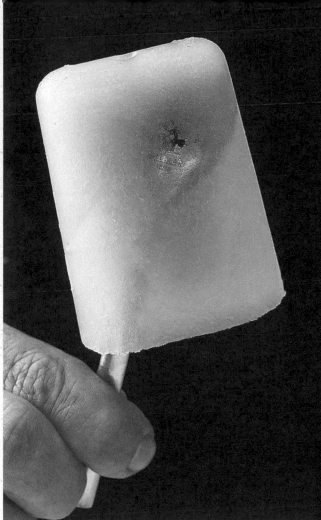

also a handy method for aubergines and courgettes. Needless to say, use only the best organic oils, or butter.

Another alternative is to make big batches of special bases for your favourite dishes – such as curries, tomato sauces for pasta, ratatouilles, vegetable stews, fruit compotes – using the basic ingredients, but possibly leaving out garlic and strong flavourings. Packs of these, say in bags or wax cartons, can be defrosted at will, cutting out much time you'd otherwise spend later sorting through, selecting and preparing for each meal over and over again.

Herbs

Herbs are not difficult to freeze fresh as they are so thin, but they can soon lose their flavour to everything else, so should be frozen in closed containers. Most are more convenient to use later and store well if chopped and mixed into water, stock or oil and frozen in ice-cube trays, then repacked as ready portion-controlled chunks. Herbs should be double-packed, for example, in a sealed bag in a closed box, so they don't cross-taint – especially basil.

Sweets

One specialised side of freezing is the frozen sweet. It is remarkably easy to make your own ice lollipops from real fruit juice. Shops sell plastic moulds – but any small plastic containers will do if given good handles. Fruit-juice ice cubes are even easier and a more child-friendly size. Then there is the gamut of wonderful fruit sorbets and ices. All these are a delicious way of getting more fruit into your diet. The juice, preferably cold-extracted, mixed with sugar – and optionally egg white in the good old days – is stirred while being frozen. You take it out, whip it and put it back several times. This makes the most wonderful appetiser, dessert and treat – and it's pretty healthy if you ignore all that sugar.

ABOVE **Freeze fruit juices into lollypops, a teaspoon makes a good handle (see recipe on page 119).**
OPPOSITE LEFT **Freeze items singly that are dry, just popping them in bags.**
OPPOSITE RIGHT **Freeze wet items and soft fruit on trays then repack, even so they may still stick together somewhat, given time.**

BOTTLING

Bottling is good from the storage point of view as, once finished, the jars can be stored almost anywhere for a long time, just like commercial bottled and canned goods. The contents remain palatable longer than frozen foods, but the method takes a great deal more effort to get right. Bottling is one stage beyond the simple 'potting', or putting into bottles and jars, of say jam or jelly, where the sugar or vinegar is the main means of preservation. Bottling involves heating the contents in their jar or bottle and sealing it quickly and efficiently so that no other preservation method is needed, though one may be employed to enhance the contents.

Bottling relies on sealing out all bacteria and yeasts from the sterilised contents. The simplest way is to heat your prepared items in their jars with the lids on, but not tight. The contents are sterilised by the heat when steam can escape; then, on cooling, the seal is first fixed by vacuum pressure holding the lid down, then reinforced by a security ring or other fastening. Such well-tried old-fashioned systems, such as Kilner jars are sometimes available and worth getting – if you can find the rubber seals that go with them.

Most modern glass jars and bottles are substantial enough for sterilising, but ensure you choose the tougher ones. It is their lids, not intended for such reuse, that make it difficult. If the lids are on tight, the jars might explode when being heated. Yet if they're not tightened up when the contents are still hot, impurities can get sucked into the cooling air gap. This makes lids theoretically difficult to use, though in fact it does not stop everything working fine in practice. You run a bigger risk of infection if you leave the lids off until after heating. The best compromise is to leave the lids on loosely during the heating process, and then screw them on more tightly while the jars are still steaming hot in the pan.

As soon as the jars have been heated for long enough, lift them out – special tongs are available, though what I do is I bale out some water and then use a thick glove. Stand them on layers of newspaper so they do not get suddenly chilled at the base, and allow them to cool slowly. One alternative or addtional way to sealing the contents is a circle of greaseproof paper, coated in beeswax or paraffin wax, fitted inside the neck and floating on top of the contents – note that the wax can fail to grip all round the edge unless it's put on very well so it may need 'repairing' as the contents shrink and cool, and a final topping off with wax (a thin layer works best) when cool to ensure an all-over waxy seal.

Bottling can be done in several ways. Filled bottles packed with warm fruits and hot syrup can be stood in an oven and cooked, but this is difficult to judge with any nicety. Bottles can be stood over boiling water and steamed. They can be pressure-cooked – and some people may use a microwave oven, though I shun that. The simplest method is to surround the jars with very hot water.

In all cases, handling nearly boiling water and glass jars requires care. Bottling can become more hazardous physically but more assured biologically if you use a pressure cooker. This does give much quicker results, but it's more risky and requires very accurate timing to get it right and not overdo it. Do not economise! Buy a modern stainless-steel pressure cooker, and read and follow the instructions precisely.

If you are preserving just fruits and not vegetables, the basic 'in hot water' bottling works well enough. All it involves is packing the fruits in water, syrup, fruit juice or similar and heating them with the lids on loosely. First clean and pre-warm all the jars, or bottles, and fill them while they're still hot; then cover the fruit with hot syrup and the lids. Surround the bottles with nearly boiling water in any suitably deep saucepan, ideally one with a perforated false floor, as in most pressure cookers. After half an hour or so, seal the bottles, remove and cool. The method can be improved to give better products. The best way is to start with cold ingredients and cold water and raise the temperature slowly over longer; then many products keep their most perfect appearance. But this has to be strictly regulated with a thermometer to work in practice and is too fiddly except for those after perfection.

Next and most practical is to start with warm – not hot – water and bring this up to not quite boiling over half an hour, then keep it there for another five to thirty minutes, depending on the product, before sealing and cooling. This is simplest, reasonably quick and gives fairly good results. Purées and other pre-cooked items need only be brought up to near-boiling point, then sealed and cooled immediately. Anything finely divided, small berries and cubed fruits need similar treatment over half an hour, plus up to five to ten minutes more. Big, chunky or lumpy fruits, such as whole small apples, plums and pears, need up to a full extra half-hour – or even more if they are old-fashioned cooking pears!

Earlier I said 'preserving just fruits and not vegetables', because although vegetables can easily be bottled they are much riskier. If fruit goes off you get fermentation and drunken headaches. If veg go off, you may get dead. The lack of acidity in vegetables makes bottling them without a back-up method inherently more risky. They are safest brined or pickled – or both – and then heat-bottled just to be sure. Indeed, almost everything pickled or preserved is best given the extra protection of bottling after potting. Not many fresh products, though, are worth bottling if you have a freezer.

TOP LEFT TO RIGHT, BOTTOM LEFT TO RIGHT Pouring warm juice onto peach halves in a proper jar for bottling. Bottling takes place with the lid loose – note tall asparagus saucepan for a tall bottle containing pears. Once the bottling is over, close the lid before cooling starts. Peaches once bottled are very like tinned ones, but better.

JUICING

Juices can be drunk or otherwise used raw, or turned into sugared syrups to be diluted for drinking or other uses. These syrups can then be preserved by bottling, but with things like apple and grape it is easier to freeze large amounts than to bottle them. I freeze them in recycled plastic bottles and waxed cartons. Juice is easily made on a small scale with a host of different kitchen appliances, and on a bigger scale with rentable wine-making gear. Drinking juice is one of the simplest ways of making your daily diet a lot healthier and, although lacking some of the fibre of the original fruit, it still has most of the goodness.

One way to get more juice over a longer time is to drink one and freeze one. Every time you make a glass of juice, make another one to freeze, in a plastic cup, for another day when that fruit is no longer fresh. Repack the labelled cups in a sealed bag once frozen.

Kitchen juicers may squeeze, centrifugally spin or suck juice out very efficiently, depending on the brand. The choice is difficult – but generally those that squeeze slowly are reckoned to keep the product cooler, so are better than those that grate and shred at high speed with a centrifuge to spin out the juice. Try different ones: look for those easy to clean, repairable and producing a clear or cloudy

juice, depending on your preference. Some are happy juicing carrots, while others are too weak for such tough, dry items. Some can deal with soft pastes, whereas others work better with pips and skins. Basically you need to find one, or more, to suit your particular uses. The cleverest I've found is a suction device, the Cecil Vacuum Press: a reversed bicycle-pump action removes the air from a container, thereby sucking the juice into it through a tube from a fine net bag of pulp; this bag is held in a mesh bag inside a bigger plastic bag, which you manipulate manually. As no heat is involved, this is very effective for fresh soft fruits, such as peaches and raspberries – but not good on hard or dry ones, such as blackcurrants or carrots! It keeps everything air-free, so the juices it makes are very good. Of course, almost anything can be heated and broken down first, with or without extra water or other juice, and then squeezed in the Cecil – but as the machine's through-put is small that seems pointless; large quantities of such pulp would be as well strained in an ordinary bag overnight.

Be warned: none of the usual kitchen juicers works at a great rate and will soon break if overworked by someone trying to fill a forty-gallon barrel rather than a few bottles. If you want to start making big batches, invest in appropriate equipment. Small-scale wine-making equipment is excellent; look for a brand made simply from stainless steel, hardwoods and cleanable plastic. I bought mine years ago and it has more than earned its keep.

Ideally, juices are made and drunk fresh – especially those of vegetable origin. But in cases such as grapes, where the crop rots, the juice needs to be made now to be frozen and drunk later. All that is needed is to stop it fermenting. Good filtering helps, as do clean fruit and hygienic handling. But these alone will still not prevent fermentation. Bottling, (see page 48), is an option, though it destroys the flavour too much for my taste – as do the majority of heat-extraction processes for obtaining the juice in the first place (although slowly heating pears to extract their juice is about the only way of using up any glut). Some juices, such as apple, are delicious with no alteration; others need additional sugar to make them palatable, and the bland may need something acid – but neither sugar nor acid is sufficient on its own to stop most juices from fermenting, unless they're bottled or frozen.

Freezing juice is the best option. I reuse plastic bottles, always under-filling them and squeezing the air out before the cap is screwed tight to make sure there's room for expansion. I freeze them upright, then store them sideways. On thawing, upright, any sediment accumulates at the bottom and the juice can be decanted off into another bottle for a clearer product. Or, if you want a concentrated juice, stop thawing when it is halfway thawed – there will be a piece of predominantly water ice left in the bottle. But usually you let juice thaw to its original strength, then keep it refrigerated – and drink it within a few days as it will ferment sooner or later.

Concentrates can be made if you simmer down a clear juice in a wide pan with no lid. The juice can be pre-reduced by being frozen first and then the ice removed when it is partly defrosted. Apple juice simmered slowly turns into a clear sweet acid syrup that sets to a jelly in the fridge, grape juice does similarly, and pear becomes a dark treacle more like maple syrup. Although these have been boiled, they may still ferment unless properly bottled and sealed, or kept in the fridge or freezer. Juice concentrates can be used not only as the basis of drinks, but also to pack fruits in for freezing or bottling, and to add sweetness to other products. Some frozen concentrates and juices, if made with too little water or with too much added sugar, may, on thawing, be found to have turned to a jam or jelly rather than a syrup as intended. This can be remedied if you heat the jelly in its bottle, slowly, in a bath of warm water.

OPPOSITE LEFT Damned expensive juicer, but it does a good job – here I'm getting carrot juice, and left over the squeezed out remains can be added to curry bases, stews, savoury or sweet, and even cakes.
RIGHT If you partly defrost a bottle of juice, you leave behind a lump of mostly ice and so concentrate the juice, making it much, much sweeter.

JAMMING AND JELLYING

The next methods are essentially all the same: preservation with sugar. The high sugar levels suck moisture out of cells, making it difficult for moulds to start growing. When this is combined with good-quality clean crops, bottling and hygiene, very high-grade produce can be made and will keep for ever – although eventually becoming more vinous and port-like until no longer palatable. Very old jam may not be tasty, but it is unlikely to be dangerous.

Jamming

This is the art of getting boiled-down fruit to set into a gel with sugar. Almost all jams work with about a fifty–fifty mix, by weight, of sugar and fruit; they need to be composed of at least half sugar to keep – but some is provided by the fruit. Only a few jams, such as blackcurrant, require any added water; the more usual problem is that the gel is too thin to set solid enough. The remedy is to add more pectin – easiest in the form of apple purée, which helps any jam to set, though it does add an apple overtone to the flavour. Often a mix of ripe and under-ripe fruits will set and taste better than ripe alone; overripe fruits rarely jam well. Another reason for poor jam is too bland a flavour; this is not corrected by the addition of more sugar but requires more acid – again supplied by apple purée, juice or concentrate, or by lemon/redcurrant/white-currant/green-grape juice called verjuice. (I keep small packs of these frozen, ready to add to jams and juices.) Of course, the addition of extra material requires extra sugar to maintain the fifty–fifty balance – not quite so much if apple concentrate is used.

One problem that has bedevilled jam-making is the notion that you can make the most jam from a limited amount of fruit and sugar by adding large amounts of water. This is, with the exception of blackcurrants, not really necessary in most cases. Some moisture left after you've washed the dust off the fruit is permissible, as is sufficient liquid to prevent catching when you're cooking down, and extra liquids as above can be added for good reasons. But plain water should rarely be needed; it dilutes the goodness too much. The second problem, arising from this first, has been the long boiling of jam to get the maximum set – just in order to get the most water combined with the fruit. Well, this is unnecessary if we are growing and preserving for our own table, and not for sale or survival. If we simply increase the amount of fruit and sugar and keep the water to a minimum, it usually sets to a semi-solid anyway. A third problem has been that, for this long boiling, huge batches were made, bubbling away in cauldrons, catching and burning at the bottom. Well, this last is even simpler to fix: it's far better to make several smaller batches in the same pan; each will be quicker, as the same surface area bubbling away will represent a lesser volume, and it will be easier to stir, pour and handle.

For goodness' sake do stir, and with a wooden spatula, especially once the sugar goes in; remember, stirring is to prevent sticking and catching, so scrape the bottom evenly and uniformly – regularly. Any breaking-up of the fruit should mostly have been done beforehand, and you don't want to make a slurry – although I do use a potato-masher to press recalcitrant lumps and unbroken berries against the bottom, before stirring again.

Indeed, that first stage is an important one for jam. When you're reducing the prepared fruit down to a pulp, the finer it is chopped/minced/sliced by hand beforehand, the quicker the breakdown when cooking. Likewise, stones in plums and so on are best removed when you're cleaning the fruits, unless you want them for their flavour. But choose the method of reduction carefully: if you mince you get a purée, if you chop you get lumps, if you slice you get thick or thin slices. The final texture will depend on how finely the fruit is prepared and how evenly. The danger is always of lumps ungelled in the middle; hence the use of the masher to press such lumps out.

The prepared fruit should be heated in a pan with a lid, and shaken and stirred to keep it from sticking. Generally add no more water (or preferably juice) other than enough initially to cover the bottom of the pan to start the breakdown. Meanwhile, the equal weight (to that of fruit plus water plus juice) of sugar should be warming up, ready to go in. But don't be too quick to add that sugar; it goes in at the very last. Bring the fruit pulp to a simmer – not a boil – keeping the lid on whenever you're not stirring, to prevent the flavour from escaping. But keep uncovering the pan to stir. Use a potato-masher to press the fruit, making sure no bits stay too solid; however, don't use the masher too vigorously as this will ruin any texture. The idea is to help the pieces give up their juices, not to reduce them to a mince.

As the fruity mix simmers, scum rises to the top. Skimming this off helps to get rid of impurities; a metal spoon will take it off neatly. A knob of butter smeared on the inside of the dry pan before you start can prevent some of the scum from forming and push any dross that does form to the wall to be scraped off. But don't be too keen to skim off what are no more than bubbles. Continue to

OPPOSITE PAGE **Use a CLEAN wooden spoon as a metal one does not prevent sticking as well. A stainless steel saucepan is best, try to avoid aluminium, copper and non-stick.**
THIS PAGE **Use a funnel to ease filling, and newspaper eases partner's angst as well as prevents jars cooling too quickly at the base. Lids on straightaway, and the labels, the labels…**

simmer until there are no more discernible solid lumps of fruit. Deliberate lumps may of course be planned, but these always threaten jam; their soft centres are a source of too much moisture, which often comes out later. Now the ready-warmed sugar can be added, slowly mixed in and carefully stirred till it has all melted; then the jam has to come back to a simmering boil. At this point you can test whether it will set: drop a little on a cold plate, it should thicken quickly, if not pop it in the freezer; after five minutes it will set if it's ready, but won't have had time to freeze. If it sets, jar immediately as the rest has cooked another five minutes anyway.

The jars are best pre-warmed in the oven, then handled carefully (I use a wooden-spoon handle first) and placed on newspaper protecting a tray. They can be filled immediately with a wide-necked jam funnel, and the cleaned hot lids put on straight after with little risk of contamination. If the jars are hot, the jam may bubble up – furiously if it's very hot. This is to be guarded against as dangerous. (But if it happens and the lid is put on as the contents finish frothing, then a very good seal is ensured and you can be confident the contents were well sterilised and boiled down slightly further as they frothed.) The jars then need to be stood somewhere to cool; that's why they are best filled on paper on a tray, as it can be moved with all of them together – ideally without jostling or shaking. Once cooled overnight, they can be inspected to see if the jam is set enough – that is, it will not run if tilted; bulging is okay but not levelling – and the lids checked. And then label the jars before anyone forgets what's in them! Remember: long, low cooking to start with, then add the sugar and quickly heat it up, put into hot jars and cover as soon as possible.

Jellying

This is essentially the same as jamming but without all the bits, so it creates a beautiful clear gel. The great advantage of jellying is where the fruit is itself very seedy, as with raspberries, or the seeds are big and irritant, as in blackberries, and thus unpleasant to some. Hence the popularity of raspberry, redcurrant, and blackberry-and-apple jellies. A clear jelly can also be used as the basis for dessert jellies and syrups, whereas a jam cannot so easily.

Making jelly means you might be just a tad lazier with the picking quality control, thinking the odd bit of stalk, leaf or whatever would not be quite so important if it were to be sieved out anyway. May I counsel against this error: quality is everything.

Starting with fresh fruits, cook them with a little more water – or preferably other juices – to get a broken-down pulp. Then strain out all the bits – the skins, stalks and seeds – to give a juice, maybe further concentrated by boiling down a bit, that can be set with about its own weight of sugar (just as for jam). If a juice is too thin, it may not set; either boil it down to remove more water, or freeze out the water as ice or combine it with a more settable juice, such as redcurrant, or with apple concentrate.

Needless to say, a coarse sieve does not make for a clear juice to produce a good jelly, so use a straining bag of fine well-washed cloth to filter the fruit pulp out of the juice. Often it will be best hung to drip overnight. Squeezing it manually, or rapidly, increases the risk of cloudiness as small bits get forced through. As an economy, some people add water to the once-strained pulp, reheat it and then get a second straining to add to the first. This is worth it only if you're desperate to get more jelly of a much lower quality. You can also use some types of kitchen juicer to reduce the pulp to a juice and a solid, or to get the last drop out of the solid part. If you do oversqueeze the bag and get a cloudy juice, standing it overnight in a cool place will often deposit a lot of the impurities, and some may float to the top. Light cloudiness will often clear later when the sugar is added, but don't rely on it.

Once the juice is boiling, scum it as for jam; this is more important with jelly. Then mix in an equal weight of sugar. Once this is dissolved, the batch needs checking for set – much more so than for jam, as with a jelly it is less certain! If you're sure it will set, pot it into hot jars. If you're not quite sure, pot it anyway; then, after cooling, if it hasn't set turn that batch into a sorbet instead – seriously. Then start another batch, making the juice more concentrated from the start, or with added apple concentrate.

A mechanically expressed fruit juice may be more difficult to gel than a strained, cooked pulp, as boiled seeds contribute considerably to the setting of some gels. This is especially so with marmalade. Generally, even if there is an alternative such as a mechanical device, I prefer not to heat fruits to get their juice, both from a nutritional and – sometimes – from a taste point of view. But heating is obviously less of a problem when the juice is going on to be used to make a jelly. However, heating should be at as low a temperature and for as short a time as just necessary before straining will work. Using juice produced by straining defrosted

TOP LEFT TO BOTTOM LEFT **A straining bag hanging overnight drips a clear juice. Squeezing the bag manually gets out more but, possibly, cloudy juice.**
TOP RIGHT TO BOTTOM RIGHT **Remaining sludge can be further squeezed, but why? Note larger quantity of now cloudier juice in bowl. Remaining pulp can be processed further into fruit leather, so don't throw it away.**

fruits suffers from the same drawback as using mechanically pressed-out juice, namely that of losing some of the fruits' goodness and setting ability, but this still works well on the whole.

Sugar extraction is my preferred way to make a juice not for jellying but for syrups and other uses. Because the sugar is in at the start, it is more difficult to boil down, but this method can still produce some very good jelly. Fresh or frozen fruit needs to be chopped or sliced – or if soft, such as raspberries, left whole – and mixed with its own weight of sugar, say two pounds of each, then left overnight in a fridge. The next day, strain the sugary juice off the pulp. Weigh the juice and pulp. Assuming you got back most of the sugar and much of the juice from the pulp (the pulp had some of its own sugar before) then the weight of pulp left, let's say a third of a pound, can be subtracted from the original weight, four pounds, to get the weight of juice and sugar extracted, which should be three and two thirds pounds. That means one and two thirds pounds of juice was extracted by, and is now mixed with, two pounds of sugar. So, in this case, the juice has just about the right amount of sugar to set for most fruits (more can be added if there's too little, or extra juice such as redcurrant or apple added if there's far too much). This syrupy juice can be frozen for later, used as a squash or cordial or made into jellies and sorbets. The pulp left can be added to jams, chutneys or wines and used in a host of other ways, but usually best is to turn it into leather (see page 41).

SYRUPS AND SQUASHES

A syrup, say blackcurrant, is really a cordial; if it has any tiny bits in it then it becomes a squash. Either is a sugary juice to which you add water to make a refreshing drink. Syrup is easiest and tastiest when made by the sugar-extraction process for getting juice out of fruit for jellying – see above. I have often made fruit-juice squashes, adding sugar syrup to sweeten them, and have later found them turned to jelly. This can be prevented by fermenting the fruit for a day or so before you add the sugar, or even by using a dubious pectin-decomposing enzyme.

But the other way to make syrups is to sweeten a raw or pressed juice. You have to add sugar, but it's difficult to get enough to dissolve without heating, so it's more effective to add sugar syrup. Fill a saucepan nearly full with sugar, then carefully add boiling water till full again, whilst stirring; stir till all the sugar dissolves, though a little may crystallise out after cooling. The resulting sugar syrup, after cooling, can be mixed with your juice, or alcoholic extract, to taste. Syrups for dilution can be made and used from the fridge as the sugar protects them, but for long-term storage they are best either bottled or frozen. Strawberry is my number-one favourite, blackcurrant and raspberry second and third.

FRUIT PRESERVES AND FREEZER JAMS

Ideally, these should be just bottled fruit in their own concentrated juice or syrup, not some nondescript jam. The fruit is retained in pieces within a gel, so there's a danger of moisture in the lumps diluting the gel. You can get around this by pre-processing the fruit, or rather by using fruit that has been dried out by sugar or alcoholic extraction for the juice. The flavour is, of course, downgraded, so using fresh fruit may be preferable. But the danger of it going mouldy is lessened with pre-processed fruits, so you can get away without bottling the lot – although once opened the preserve should be used quickly. Or you can make freezer jam: you know it won't keep so you simply freeze it until required, then keep it in the refrigerator and use it up in a matter of days before it can go off. Plastic not glass jars, of course! Freezer jelly is effectively a sorbet.

FRUIT CHEESES AND BUTTERS

These are a form of high-fruit, low-sugar jams – in fact very similar to a soft leather, though not taken so far. A cheese is as firm as cheese, and may be eaten by the chunk; a butter is used more like jam from the jar and is really almost indistinguishable from it. Often made from strongly flavoured highly acidic wild fruits and berries to be eaten with fatty game, these cheeses and butters need maturing for some months till required. Quince cheeses are the original marmalade (they're still made in Spain and Portugal), quite substantial and eaten in chunks. Damsons and medlars are also made into cheeses and butters; apples rarely except as fillers. Often spices are included, and sugar added – up to the same amount as for jam. Cheese is made in the same way as jam, with a thicker, drier purée with only the coarsest parts removed – much like the pulp used for a leather. This is then cooked long and slow, until a dab on a plate does not separate out any 'juice'. Unlike leather, a cheese has sugar added – about half to three quarters as much as for jam – and it's not as cooked down or as dried as leather, but in blocks or cartons is in a much firmer state than jam. Fruit butter is like a cheese but still spreadable, so is potted in jars, as for jam.

OPPOSITE LEFT **The finest flavours are captured with sugar extraction or preservation... and forget the calories.**

CANDYING AND CRYSTALLISING

This is fiddly, but worth it for a few garnishes with which you can add your own flourishes, such as candied violet and rose petals and citrus peel. Crystallised and candied fruits are hardly a staple but they're a nice treat. First, the fruit is candied – most commonly cherries and apricots, choice plums, peaches and ripe pears, but anything may be worth attempting; I do my own ginger.

When you've chosen your fruits, halve and stone them, peel the skins off or prick them all over with a pin; with pears, just peel and halve them. Boil them in minimal water and/or apple concentrate or their own juice, just long enough to soften them without letting them break down, say five to ten minutes. Then allow them to cool in their own juices, and refrigerate overnight. Next day, pour off the juice and add sugar at the rate of 12oz to a pint (340g to 600ml), bring to the boil and pour it over the fruit; then leave to soak for another day.

The next day, drain the syrup off, add another 4oz (110g) sugar per pint (600ml), bring to the boil and again pour it over the fruit, leave to soak, and again the next day, and the next, adding another 4oz to each pint each day for a week or so, by which time the syrup should be getting very thick when cold. From this point, boil the fruit in the syrup for four or five minutes each day before putting it aside to soak overnight. After a fortnight or so of this, the fruits turn clear; drain them and set aside to dry in a warm, dry place, then coat them with sugar and pack in jars or tins – or coat them with melted chocolate, which I reckon is the neatest method.

For skinny items, such as petals, dip each one alternately in strong sugar solution and caster sugar to build up a crust, allowing it to dry with each layer. (Some people use glucose or dextrose to replace part of the sugar, as it gives a better finish.)

The syrup left over from making each sort of candied fruit can be made into a delicious sauce, or sorbet, or syrup squash – or probably best of all turned into a liqueur by the addition of overproof white rum or other tipple. Or it can be combined with icing sugar to make fruit fondant for topping cakes, spreading between biscuits or filling your own chocolates.

Chocolate-coating candied fruits is not only scrumptious self-indulgence but a genuine method of preservation, as the chocolate coating makes each bit more handleable, packable and durable while sealing the fruit within from any slight dampness about. Slowly melt some chocolate – organic, of course – in a bowl over a saucepan of boiling water. Dip the chilled candied dried fruits, each stuck on the end of a cocktail stick, into the chocolate, slowly rotating until covered, then withdraw slowly and allow to drip, and then cool. Simple aids for this last task include using the ubiquitous cheese-and-pineapple-on-sticks method: take a large potato or apple, cut it in half and lay the halves flat on plates so you can push one end of the cocktail stick in while the chocolate fruit cools on the other. Perfectionists will seal the hole where the stick is withdrawn with a drop more chocolate. Alternatively, the coated pieces can be set to cool laid on oiled wire trays, or even on plates well covered with icing or caster sugar.

These chocolate-coated fruits can even be frozen to make them last longer. Or you can seal your dried fruit and chopped blanched nuts in slabs of chocolate, simply by stirring the dried or crystallised or alcohol-soaked fruits into melted chocolate and then pouring this into an oiled lined tray to set. A better seal and finish is obtained if you first pour in a thin layer of chocolate to coat the bottom and sides of the tray and let that set in a freezer. Then into the cold mould pack the still warm fruit and nut and chocolate mixture and smooth it flat. Once that has firmed up, seal the mixture under another thin layer of pure chocolate. You can even make individual chocolates using this same process, repeating it using special trays like egg boxes with many small depressions. Line these all at once by pouring in melted chocolate, letting it partly set and then pouring off the surplus to leave a thin coating. Leave this to set in the freezer where it will harden quickly. Then give each cell or depression its own filling – a bit of home-made marzipan (finely ground nuts and sugar), candied fruit, nuts, fruit fondant, liqueured or dried fruit – and seal the tray over with another layer of melted chocolate. Once this has set cold and hard, in the freezer preferably, remove the whole piece from the tray and break off the individual truffles or whatever and pack them suitably.

There is no limit to this method: you can have mint-sauce-coated green peas in chocolate if you want. I found it was a good way of making lemon-meringue pie more transportable (see page 120) – or you could have a soft meringue marshmallow layer sealed under yet another layer of chocolate. I'm fond of mince-pie-filled chocolates at Christmas, and rather perversely sage-and-onion-stuffing ones too! As I said there are no limits – as appetisers, try dark chocolates with pickled-anchovy-and-hazelnut-meringue centres.

PICKLES, CHUTNEYS, SAUCES AND KETCHUPS

All of these are comestibles preserved in vinegar, and jams in which vinegar and salt add to the preservative actions of sugar and bottling. The majority of sweet pickles are small bits of vegetable in a sweet-and-sour sauce of some sort, based on two pounds of sugar in every pint of vinegar (900g in every 600ml). So

PAGE 58 TOP LEFT TO RIGHT Chocolate melting in a bain marie with nuts and dried fruit. Melted chocolate mix spooned into frozen chocolate lined tray of cups. Chocolate mix does not quite fill lined cups.
BOTTOM LEFT TO RIGHT Filled cups are put back in the freezer. Filled chilled cups are now finished with another layer of melted chocolate and put back in the freezer. Frozen chocolates being banged out of the tray of cups.
PAGE 59 With a little trim these are soon finished (off).

RIGHT Pickled cucumbers are nothing without dill.
BELOW You can have culinary delights unknown in the supermarket.

TOP LEFT TO RIGHT Boil beetroot in their skins with the leaf stalks twisted off. Once boiled, cool then top and tail and slip the skins off.
BOTTOM LEFT TO RIGHT Slice straight into a part-filled jar of vinegar. Add more vinegar to completely cover the slices.

sweet-corn relish is simply bits of sweet corn in a sweet-and-sour onion-and-apple jam with a little hot chilli. If flavoured with tamarind paste, dates and pepper, it becomes a brown sauce. If – either instead or as well – you add curry powder or other spice, then it becomes a chutney. Thus, tomato ketchup is a thin sweet-and-sour tomato jelly or butter.

The essential thing is to keep the moisture levels down, so use strong vinegar and sufficient sugar. Use only good-quality fresh spices, as old ones give off flavours and cause moulds. All pickles rely on their acid ingredients to discourage moulds, but the vinegar and salt also attack metal so it is best to use glass containers with plastic lids. Plastic lids cannot be left on or put on if the jars are heated for bottling, so use temporary paper covers and replace these with the plastic lids before cooling. If you need to use metal lids, then melt beeswax on the undersides before use to give them some protection.

Pickles

Many of the best pickles are simple, such as onions or nasturtium seeds, which are no more than cleaned, brined (see page 64) and soaked in spiced vinegar – simple as that. Some people even dispense with the brining and just cover whatever with sufficient vinegar to effect good storage. To pickle beetroots, boil, peel and slice them and drop them in vinegar. Bottling as well may help, but is not often necessary where sufficient vinegar is used to cover all the ingredients generously. Pickles need storing in the cool and dark and, as noted above, plastic lids last longer!

Although brining is usually done cold, you can boil the vinegar and pour it over the vegetables, soak overnight, then drain and repeat; this can improve the colour or texture more than just soaking in cold vinegar.

There is quite a choice as to which vinegar to use: malt vinegar as used for chips is the one for many traditional pickles – onions, beetroot and so on. Spirit or distilled vinegar is clear and has no malt flavour, and is better for preserving vegetables that want to keep their flavour or colour. Ready-spiced pickling vinegar is the same, flavoured with the manufacturer's choice of cheap spices at a premium. 'Non-brewed condiment' is the cheap gubbins you put on your chips in a bad establishment – it is totally synthetic and may well mess up your insides!

Cider and wine vinegars are another choice, with different flavours suited to different pickles – or tastes. Mint sauce is best with malt or cider vinegar, but mustard with wine vinegar. Balsamic vinegar is simply pre-flavoured and salted – it makes a good salad dressing, though.

Sweet pickles are bits of fruit or vegetable in a fruit jam with vinegar and maybe some chilli for piquancy. Many of the ingredients for sweet pickles may be brined and then vinegared first. Often you can help the vinegar or jam to set by adding in cornflour, as for a custard.

Many other pickles are similar, with the sauce and main ingredients being whatever takes your fancy, or whatever is surplus. My mother used to make a walnut-and-runner-bean pickle – or was it a chutney?

Chutneys

These odd Anglo-Indian concoctions are useful for converting surplus fruits and vegetables into a storable commodity. Similar to many pickles, chutneys often have apple purée and onions as a common base, boiled with sugar, vinegar and not inconsequential salt; this is combined with almost any other fruit or vegetable mixture. Plums, tomatoes and peaches are good choices, but almost anything is possible. Mince or finely chop your basic ingredients, retaining only dried fruits as whole pieces. You can give the mixture zest with ginger and other spices, especially allspice, chilli, cayenne, curry and cumin. Traditionally, raisins and sultanas – home-dried, of course – and dates are almost essential. Garlic is sometimes included. Brown sugar is used for dark chutneys, though long cooking will also darken the mix. The vinegar is usually malt, but spirit or cider vinegar make good alternatives with some ingredients. Potting (putting into bottles or jars) is usually sufficient, but bottling is safer. Chutneys are a great favourite with cold meats and in sandwiches with cheese.

Sauces and Ketchups

As mentioned before, the commonest of these, tomato sauce, catsup, ketchup or whatever, is no more than thin tomato jelly or paste with vinegar, a lot of sugar and some spices added – more a sort of runny chutney. Remarkably popular and apparently better for us than fresh tomatoes, the commercial product is of a quality that is hard to match; but making ketchup is a good way of storing some more tomatoes. Of course, you need not make the sauce, only the purée, and bottle that – though you may as well add basil, thyme, bay or oregano and so on anyway, and bottle or freeze batches of your tomatoes as pasta sauce bases instead.

Tomatoes are not the only ketchup base; plum sauce is very similar and used to be popular, as was mushroom ketchup. As with pickles and chutneys, the various sauces and ketchups are flavoured with spices to make brown sauces, hot or piquant, mustardy sauces and so on. Then there are other sauces, such as horseradish, mint and so on that are effectively more like pickles.

SALTING

Once, salted foods – especially meat – were commonplace; now very little is salted solely so it will keep, although many foods are salted or brined as part of another process, if only to stop browning from exposure to air. Some watery vegetables are salted to reduce their water content rapidly and so aid preservation. You can cut cucumbers and marrows into slices or cubes and mix these with salt in a plastic or glass container, then stand them for a day or so in the cool. Then strain them from the brine they form, and wash and rinse them until they're desalted enough to be pickled with vinegar. The only vegetable still commonly salted seems to be sliced green beans.

Salted beans

Use either French or runner beans picked young and tender. Top and tail them, slice them if they're of any width, then mix them with salt in the ratio of three to one by weight. Pack the mixture carefully, tamping it down, into jars with plastic lids. If these are kept cool, the salt turns to brine as the beans give up their water and shrink, and within a week the jars can be topped up with more bean and salt mixture, and possibly once again a third time. Always make sure the beans are covered by brine or a layer of salt, and keep the jars cool and securely closed till required. Before use, the beans need to be washed several times to get rid of the salt, then soaked in warm water for an hour or two before you change it again and boil them as if fresh.

BRINING

As mentioned on page 62, we often brine vegetables to prepare them for pickling. It is gentler than salting. Immersing the washed prepared vegetables in a strong brine of a pound of salt to every gallon of water (500g to every 5 litres) sucks out some of the moisture and kills many bacteria and fungi. It also very effectively dislodges bigger bugs from inside things like cauliflower florets. Food-grade plastic bowls are most convenient, with plastic trays to weight down the floaters. Commercially treated vegetables may be held for months or years, but for home pickling, brining for a few days is sufficient. Then the vegetables can be drained, rinsed and further processed while still in top condition. Few vegetables will remain in the same condition if just brined. Long-term brining changes them over months, as a slow lactic-acid fermentation takes place which cures vegetables, turning them a different shade of colour, and they become more transparent. This is one reason why home-made pickle is rarely the same as bought.

Sauerkraut fermentation

I must say at this point that I do not like sauerkraut much; indeed I could never see any again with little sadness. This is not improved by my having gone, while writing this, to check on some sauerkraut in my stores – only to find it had synchronously erupted after years of quiescence and made a right old mess. However, sauerkraut does remain a unique way of keeping some food in case of dire famine. More akin to yogurt or beer than to something like beans merely preserved in salt, it is a fermented product. To make it, mix shredded cabbage and salt together at a (much more dilute) rate of thirty-two to one, pack into large glass or glazed jars and then – unlike for a cool salt dehydration – leave it to ferment at a warm room temperature, say 70–80°F (20–25°C). Use a weighted wooden or plastic lid to press all the cabbage just under the brine, which you should top up with more brine, made at half an ounce per pint (15g per 600ml), as it proceeds to rot – sorry, ferment. Anyway, as it ferments, a scum floats up which needs skimming off. After a few weeks, when it has stopped fermenting, it can be eaten, or heated and bottled for later use.

OPPOSITE LEFT **French beans being sliced with wee gadget (that always chops my finger too so be careful).**
OPPOSITE TOP RIGHT **Sliced beans and bits of finger being mixed with generous amounts of salt.**
OPPOSITE BOTTOM RIGHT **Very salty mixture packed into jars, which will dissolve down and can have more added in a week.**

CIDER AND WINE

I start with cider, as it is, in practice, the easiest of all the home-brewing options, and a really tasty good-quality wine is easier to make from apples than from grapes. (I am aware this will probably annoy some people who have not yet tried a good cider and know only awful commercial and rough stuff.) Wine, and very palatable wine, is also easily achievable at home from grapes, to say little of all the other fruits that can be turned into quite satisfying drinks with little more effort. But cider can be the best, and apples are easy to come by.

The same degree of hygiene is needed for brewing as for preserving by any other means, indeed all the more so as the same equipment is reused so often and possibly not washed as well. Hygiene is even more important if the same equipment is used for producing juices for storing, as then any contamination is more of a problem than in juice destined for fermenting, anyway.

Cider

You do not have to become an alcoholic to appreciate a daily glass of cider, and it is one of the tastier ways of storing a surplus crop of apples. First of all I suggest you aim not at a traditional scrumpy or cloudy cider, but at a fine wine akin to a light dry white that a grape will give. Then you do not need cider apples – these are sweet and very acid and ideal for the traditional ciders, but a mixture of almost any cookers and dessert apples makes a good cider, anyway. It's all in the preparation, and then the fermentation.

The apples need to be washed and prepared. I remove every bruise, as well as any rot or damage; only fruit good enough to eat goes in. Then the apples need to be minced, chopped or somehow reduced to a coarse pulp. Various methods have been used, from turnip and beet choppers to converted mangles and garden shredders, but little beats the stainless-steel and nylon geared crusher I bought two decades or more ago from a vineyard supplier. This is mounted in an old table frame for ease, and is used for crushing grapes and other fruits when it's not being used for apples. It's very easy to keep clean – I'd recommend anything similar. Likewise, a press can be used: I've had a huge wood-and-iron press, and used all sorts of others, big and small, including a simple little slatted-barrel press as sold for small-scale grape-pressing, which was excellent and, most importantly, easy to keep clean –

though I did have to replace all the screws in the slats with stainless-steel ones! Again, this was mounted on a small table for ease.

Anyway, the cleaned, prepared, crushed apple pulp needs to be squeezed, and as soon as possible. Surprisingly, the slats in the barrel soon pack with bits of peel, pips and so on, and the juice is filtered through the pulp on the way out and is pretty clean. Apple pulp pressed between boards with a bottle jack is usually wrapped in a cotton cloth first. For my big press, a billiard-frame-type arrangement was laid on a board, a cloth laid over it and the pulp poured in and levelled; then the cloth was folded and smoothed over and the frame removed, and the next board placed on top, and so on. With such an arrangement you can press a lot of juice – but it takes a long time to fill, so some of it starts to go off, and the cloths need washing between sessions. For home use I certainly now recommend that people stick to smaller batch sizes done more often; the quality is so much easier to maintain. Mind you, some good cider I once tried was made from juice extracted using a washing-machine spin dryer!

As soon as the juice is expressed, strain it, and put any wanted for freezing into plastic bottles, not quite full, squeezing them as you cap them to expel air and so allow room for expansion. The first run and last run are never the finest, so are often relegated to cider for which they are fine. Now this needs to be fermented in any sterile container – glass demijohns of about a gallon (5 litres) are a handy size, though bigger is sometimes more convenient. The important thing is they must be sterile and taint-free and equipped with some way of keeping air out, or more importantly keeping the vinegar fly with stray yeasts out. Proper bungs and traps are sold, but I find a wad of cotton wool works as well and is simpler. Another important part, though, is not just obtaining a clean apple juice but using an already fermenting white-wine-type yeast to start it, thus overwhelming the natural yeasts introduced on the apple skins. The temperature needs to be reasonably warm for fermentation, but if it's too hot it will cause off flavours; the living room is better than the airing cupboard.

FROM LEFT TO RIGHT Washed apples are cut and rotten bits removed then chopped finely. Chopped apple is poured into a small grape press. Pressure is applied, relaxed, applied, relaxed until the juice is all expressed. A sieve will catch any bits that escape.

ABOVE Picking grapes is always a pleasure.
OPPOSITE Grapes may be made into wine – but homemade raisins or just juice may be better.

The biggest cause of off flavours, however, is ill attempts to make the cider too strong. Now, there is no harm in adding sugar to boost the natural strength so the cider will keep well, but making it too strong results in off tastes. Good wine is 10% or maybe 11% alcohol, beer has 2%–6% but keeps because of pasteurisation and hops. Cider naturally comes out at about 7–8% and is good at that strength but does not keep well; adding another pound or so of sugar to a gallon (500g to 5 litres) gives cider the strength of wine. Add more than a couple of pounds and you make a heady brew with off flavours. You can make the increase exactly by using a hydrometer to measure the sugar content of the starting juice; this will tell you your final strength when it has finished fermenting, and thus you can calculate how much sugar you need to add to bring the strength up to any desired level. However, do not add that sugar early on but towards the end of the fermentation, and add it very slowly and carefully, preferably dissolved in more apple juice, as the main contents will bubble up as the new sugars mix in. Be warned: it will all be on the floor if you add it too fast. And be careful if doing big batches. Many viticulteurs have been killed by breathing the intoxicating rush coming off rapidly fermenting vats – it's heady stuff – and then falling in!

Once the fortified cider has finished fermenting, the dregs need to be poured off or they will taint it. You can do this into any corkable wine or even plastic bottles; however, it's best not to use screw-top glass bottles as any further fermentation could prove dangerous. I prefer a sparkling wine, so I put my cider in pressure bottles such as for champagne and some beers, and into plastic lemonade bottles which work well too. As I fill each one, I add a small spoonful of honey, apple concentrate or syrup which causes a final fermentation in the bottle, a fizzy drink – and a small amount of sediment. This last can be got round on opening by careful decanting – or by the champagne method, which is a tedious if clever trick: the bottles are given their secondary fermentation but turned upside down and rotated till all the sediment has collected in the hollow cap; the necks of the bottles are then frozen so that a plug of ice retains the contents, and then the hollow cap and dregs can be removed and exchanged for a proper cork, wired on. Voila!

Unlike most wines, cider does not take long to mature, and that made in the autumn can be drunk at the winter celebrations – but it is best the following year. I have saved some for decades now and I can tell you it does not improve with age (unlike some wines, which have surprised me).

Now can you likewise make pear cider from dessert pears rather than perry pears? Well, it seems to me, no – or at least I have not yet got the knack. The first problem is that dessert pears get too soft; if they're ripe they ooze out of the press like toothpaste, and if they're unripe they squeeze properly but are less sweet. The next drawback is that dessert pears seem to have too much flavour; my pear-cider attempts have had too many acid-drop-like overtones to be considered pleasant.

Wine

Grapes are only too easy to turn into wine, but to get a palatable one is difficult, and to get a great one – well, not very achievable. The biggest handicap is the grape varieties on offer, which are a disease-prone lot at best! Of nearly five dozen varieties I've now grown, only a few are good and reliable producers of tasty grapes and not prone to mildew, botrytis and other plagues. That all said, it has proved remarkably easy to produce drinkable red, white and rosé wines from grapes, the only proviso being that your patience as a brewer needs to be as great as a gardener's.

Red wines are made from red grapes, skins and all, crushed and started with a suitable yeast, although they come with several, anyway. Some varieties are teinturier and have red juice as well, so

give a redder wine. The crushed grapes, stalks and all, are best fermented in suitable casks with big lids so the lot can be removed for pressing. After several weeks, squeeze the fermented crushed grapes and skins and add any sugar to bring the wine up to strength with a second fermentation, now in smaller barrels or glass demijohns. (See under cider for how to increase strength by adding sugar.) Once it's finished, drain the wine off the dregs, place in clean bottles and cork. So the cork can set, first stand the bottles upright, then later lay them on their sides; a cool cellar is ideal – but yes, you've guessed it, a dead refrigerator in a cool shed or garage will do nicely.

Most dessert and indoor-grown grapes do not make good wine, being too sweet and not acid enough, whilst with many outdoor grapes it's vice versa, so by blending them you can achieve good results. White wine can be made from red skinned grapes if you squeeze out the clear juice to ferment, but it is usually made from white or yellow grapes. And as these are usually squeezed before fermentation, no big vats are needed as they are for red grapes; all operations can be done with glass demijohns or similar. Of course, for a higher-tannin wine you can ferment the whites with their pips and skins, but I prefer to transfer those to my 'mixed red' to give it more body. A white-wine yeast instead of a red is obviously better. White wine also matures a bit more quickly than red, but can still take ages.

Another economy is to ferment the pips and skins from pressed-for-juice grapes with the next batch of red grapes, adding to their bulk and flavour. Or you can get a second squeezing out of your pips and skins by freezing them then re-squeezing, but be careful not to make the 'pips squeak' or they give a taint.

Rosé wine is also easy. I especially recommend the variety 'Siegerrebe', which is not only delicious as a dessert grape but makes an exquisite, heavily perfumed sweet wine.

All of these wines benefit from ageing in the bottle for at least a year or ten. I joke not: some reds that I put away as too harsh have mellowed into delightful quaffs after a decade or more. One reason I now stick to cider and drink the grape juice is that the former is ready so reasonably quickly.

An economy not allowed is using poor grapes: any grossly under-ripe, mouldy – or, worse, dirty – will taint the final product so must be left out. Watch out for grapes looking fine but with shrivelled shanks to the bunch; these are often bitter and should be left out.

Fruit wines from other fruits can be created in much the same manner. Some fruits, such as gooseberries and redcurrants, can be crushed and squeezed in the same way as white grapes, while others such as strawberry and raspberry have to be treated more like red grapes – although in their case they need straining bags rather than presses to separate the fermented pulp from the wine. Most do not keep unless sugar is added; most require an extra couple of pounds per gallon (1kg per 5 litres). If wine is made from things like pea pods or rhubarb which contain precious little natural sugar, then up to three and a half pounds of sugar (1.6kg) may be needed. Raisins can be substituted to some extent for sugar, at a ratio of three for two by weight – honey also, but this does add a meady overtone. There is no end to the ingenuity, or desperation, of amateur wine-makers in their recipes; almost everything not poisonous has been tried and attested as delicious by someone.

LIQUEURS

Most know of sloe gin: sloes, our wild plums, are gathered, washed, pricked and popped into bottles filled with gin and sugar. These are stored in the cool and dark and agitated weekly. The thick dark red liqueur that is poured off some months later is a good and warming drink. But the sloes left over are not much use. However, you can make liqueurs very easily from other fruits, such as apricot, plum and damson – and even make wild strawberry, blackcurrant (see photographs) and herb liqueurs, as well. And what you get left after straining off your liqueur are alcohol- or alcohol-and-sugar-soaked fruits most suitable for making delicious cakes, trifles and other desserts, blending into jams and marmalades, putting into home-made chocolates, candying or just eating as sweeties.

You can look at this the other way round and see it as a way of preserving your fruits and getting a liqueur into the bargain. There is no better or more delicious way of preserving apricots than by stuffing a jar with them, covering them with brandy, leaving them to steep for months and then repacking them in their brandy juice mixed with equal amounts of sugar syrup. Or if you are after softer, less chewy fruits, gently cook them in their own fruit juice, add an equal volume of sugar syrup to the juice and bring back to the boil, then allow to cool. Pack the fruit into jars or bottles and cover with a fifty–fifty mix of spirit and the juice/sugar mix. However, the main aim when you're making liqueurs is to get a fruit extract with as many of the nutrients and vitamins as possible, then to make that more palatable with sugar.

The traditional 'all in one go' from the start that puts all the ingredients in a bottle is different from a two-part process. Here the alcoholic extraction of the fruits takes place first, with the sugar added as syrup later once the fruit has been strained off. This gives a different product with more flavour. Or, of course, you can even leave the fruit in after adding the sugar syrup – may I point out to the miserly that gifting a bottle of home-grown fruits in their

fruit liqueur (bought spirit and bought sugar) is a lot cheaper in terms of expensive imports than gifting that same bottle full of just the home-made fruit liqueur.

The choice of fruit to steep for liqueur is obviously a personal one; however, as for wines, a blend of the sweet and the acid is often better. The choice of alcohol also makes different liqueurs – gin or brandy being traditional, whisky and oddly vodka giving less pleasing flavours to some fruits, though they are good with herbs. I find overproof white rum to be the best alcohol for steeping, as it is almost sweet and has the least overpowering flavour; vodka has a chemical taste to it by comparison. For preserving quickly: just pop the fruits, herbs or vegetables in a jar and cover them with neat overproof spirit – works every time. And always welcome as a gift. But you don't have to stop with the usual – the various edible wild fruits make interesting liqueurs once well sweetened, and the alcoholic extracts of various herbs, flowers and seeds are valuable both medicinally and culinarily.

FRUIT VINEGARS

Of course, if we are talking medicinally, you can have fruit vinegars: these combine the health benefits of both fruit and vinegar, without any alcohol – and yet they store nearly as well as liqueurs, and disappear less easily. The fruit – often blackcurrants, raspberries or blackberries – needs to be chopped or sliced and steeped in its own weight of vinegar, preferably cider or spirit, for up to a week. Then strain it, weigh it, add an equal weight of sugar, bring to a near boil and then simmer for ten minutes before bottling. Likewise if you adore pickled onions and garlic, try pickling them in fifty–fifty malt vinegar and rum! And while we are on an alcoholic fantasy, try coleslaw made with mayonnaise and white rum.

LOVE POTIONS

I am very pleased with my attempts at making my own Drambuie; this classic liqueur I long found good for my throat after public speaking. Unable to swallow the cost – or ignore a challenge – I experimented, and a good replica is had by steeping rosemary and sage flowers with twice as many thyme flowers in whisky, strained and later sweetened with honey. Flowers can be very potent. My favourite of all time, though, is violet liqueur. You make this by collecting thousands of violet petals (I jest not), removing the white bit at the base of each, carefully steeping the petals and then filtering them out and adding sugar syrup. Oddly, when you drink the liqueur the smell is imperceptible, but when you breathe the warmth out again you get the whole gamut of fragrance. It was said to be a love potion in olden times – should prove popular now, then.

coping with gluts

Coping with gluts

There are many different crops, some almost guaranteed and others sporadic in their yields; either category usually as dependent on the season as on our skill. And each gardener has their favourite, and their favourite methods of coping. In the following directory of recommended ways and means, and recipes, I deal with my choices for each subject. Of course, you may differ, and rank other methods or ways preferable. One may add more vegetables to one's diet by freezing or drying and then boiling them, or by pickling them, and more fruits by drying or by juicing, whichever is to your taste. I have chosen my most useful crops to concentrate on, and the ways that, in my experience, work.

Because of the likelihood of gluts, the need to get them away from the birds and the value, variety and ease of their processing, I must deal with the fruits first; then nuts, mushrooms, the herbs and their associates the salads, and finally vegetables.

Note that the general guidelines and safety measures for the different methods of processing and storage are detailed elsewhere (and cross-referenced here) to save unnecessary repetition.

Fruits: pomes, stones, soft, sundry

It's hard to judge what crop you may want, need or get in five or ten years' time! Yet that is what you have to do when planting fruit trees. True, they can crop before then, be transplanted or propagated or even follow you around in huge tubs. But fruit trees carry on cropping year after year, you inherit someone else's or your expectations alter. It is very likely you will have a glut most years and then occasionally no crop at all. Do plant wisely – it is easier to use up vast quantities of apples than it is of pears, and a few quinces are enough for most families. It suits more people's tastes to produce, process and consume masses of apricots preserved in different ways than it does of peaches or plums, and both those before damsons.

Soft fruit is less of a problem as it is less long-lived, and most can be processed easily, but soft fruit does need a cage or nets for success. As top fruit is long-lived, the best varieties do not change quickly so can be recommended, unlike some soft fruits and vegetables, of which few varieties persist for anywhere near as long and are nearly out of date as soon as mentioned.

Although everyone has their own tastes and fancies, there are limits to what you can use. Again, remember, if you are planning on preserving or storing a crop, you don't want to bloat it up with too much water; by all means water well till ripening starts, but then give only just enough moisture to prevent drought. If you are after only the juice, this still applies, as you still don't want to risk the fruit splitting or moulding.

POMES

The best-known in this family are apples and pears; they are related to roses and to many other garden plants that have common or similar diseases and pests. However, they mostly crop prodigiously with little or no care, thrive on most sites if the right local variety is chosen and are among the longest-storing fruits.

Apples (*Malus domestica*)

Apples are so freely grown, store so simply for many months and crop so heavily we have naturally found many ways of using them. Indeed, along with potatoes, onions, carrots and cabbage they are the backbone of our winter-to-spring domestic economy. Fresh, a good apple such as a russet can be eaten skin, core, pips and all. (Not tried it? Go on.) Then there are all the puddings and desserts, the sauces and curries and the usefulness of apple purée and concentrate for jams and jellies. Apple juice is refreshing and healthy, and remarkably easy to produce in quantity, and the fermented juice is cider – even better. Ferment it further and you have your own vinegar.

Apples can be grown in most soils and on most sites, and the trained forms fitted to walls and fences even if there is no room for bushy or standard trees. Most apple varieties and rootstocks are not awfully happy confined in containers, but some special varieties can be so grown if you have little choice, or if you wish to force earlier or carry later crops under cover. There are even almost bonsai-size potted patio-table varieties that carry full-size fruits.

If you have the choice, plant many varieties, all as cordons or small trees, rather than have the labour-saving fewer standards, as a greater number spreads the risks of gluts and failures and ensures pollination (rarely a problem for apples with so many about anyway) – and, of course, more variety is more interesting. So make the choices what you will, preferably local varieties, but I'd recommend planting only one – or, at most two or three – early dessert apples; these have least value as they go over and become

OPPOSITE **Plums often break their branches with heavy gluts.**

unusable almost as soon as picked ('Discovery' is probably the best). And do plant any dessert apples as dwarf trees that produce small crops, as a glut of these fruits is not convenient.

The most useful trees to have are late keepers, especially really late storing cookers as these are expensive to buy and hard to scrump. Then you want tasty late storing desserts that keep for months, up to Easter at least, particularly one or two russets. Plant only a small selection of midseason desserts or cookers, those you really crave and can't find, because there are enormous quantities of apples about for the asking if simple bulk for processing is required. However, to ensure sheer bulk for juicing or processing it is hard to beat a few trees of such a strong grower as 'Bramley's Seedling', plus a pollinator or two, on strong stocks left to get huge. Growing them through grass reduces yields a tad but gives the best keepers, as grass left to grow unchecked as the crop ripens up robs the trees of water and nitrogen, making the fruit store better – and incidentally making it redden more – and the long grass cushions windfalls.

Thinning and pruning

Ruthless fruit-thinning early on, and repeated a couple of times, reduces apple pests and diseases more than most other measures. Knocking off all mummified apples in deep winter is another valuable remedy. Wood ashes are needed by old trees, and especially by the cookers, and will give a much cleaner, better-storing crop. And a shortage of lime may cause fruits to have internal spotting. As with most crops, plenty of moisture while they're growing, but less when they're ripening, and doses of seaweed sprays will benefit the yields and quality.

Pruning trained trees needs to be completely opposite from pruning 'natural' trees. The latter, whether small or large growing, are best left entirely alone save for remedial work – that is in winter, when you can see what's what, remove any dead, diseased, damaged and misdirected (growing too close or towards other) branches. Trained apple trees, whether cordons, espaliers or goblet-shaped dwarfs, all need hard pruning IN SUMMER. You can use shears to remove three quarters of every shoot, saving only those needed to extend the framework, and in winter repeat the same again but even more severely and ruthlessly. There is a problem with a few varieties: called tip-bearers, these do not fruit on spurs on the branches as do most apples (and pears, gooseberries, redcurrant, whitecurrant and grapes), but on the ends of the shoots that grew last year. Because of this habit they are hard to train, and have to be left to make 'natural' heads and then just

remedially pruned – and never sheared all over.

The harder you prune, the less wood is left and the fewer buds and fewer fruits in total – which then each get larger. Even so, most apple trees still overcrop and set too many fruits – sometimes causing them to exhaust themselves and take a year off. Most naturally have what is called the June drop when, in early summer, the trees reassess their ability and drop surplus fruitlets, retaining only as many as they can ripen – but that is ripen seeds, the important bit from the trees' point of view. We, however, want fewer, bigger, cleaner fruits, not vast numbers of small seedy ones; thus the value of fruit-thinning to the kitchen. If you go over the swelling crop several times and remove many substandard fruitlets, the rest will be much better. THE TOTAL WEIGHT CROPPED DOES NOT GO DOWN MUCH BUT THE QUALITY IS VASTLY IMPROVED. This is extremely important for the storing of apples: if infected, infested, cracked, blemished, misshapen, congested and ill-placed fruits are removed from the tree and hygienically buried or burned, not only are all those fruits left to be later picked much more likely to store well, but many future

BELOW **Too beautiful to waste, yet windfalls will not keep – process them straightaway.**

problems will also have been defused. And which would you rather peel and slice – two hundred small or seventy huge apples?

I cannot overemphasise the value of good thinning if you want to store them; however, if you are going to process the bulk it is not so important – except from the point of view of year-on-year production. When the tree ripens many small fruits, obviously far more seeds are ripened than with fewer, bigger fruits. The seeds take vastly more fats, proteins, minerals and nutrients than does the sugary pappy flesh we eat, and so it is the number of seeds that exhaust the tree, not the weight of crop. Thinning the crop can hardly be overdone, but be careful not to thin once and heavily just before heavy rains come as this may cause the remainder to split.

When thinning, go over each tree several times rather than all in one attempt, as this will reduce the shock and danger of splits. I re-iterate, it is hard to over-thin; no matter how vicious you are, it is amazing how the final result fills out. First remove the obviously diseased or infested, misshapen, holed or cracked fruits, and burn or bury them promptly along with all fallen ones. Then remove the centre or 'king' fruit of each bunch, then several more; three left together will probably be too crowded unless no others at all are within a good hand's breadth. Take more of those from the shade and centre, and leave more in full sun. Some of the late storers, such as 'Winston' and 'Tydeman's Late Orange', are very prone to producing masses of small fruits – thin these really hard – while 'Charles Ross' and 'Norfolk Beauty' often make large fruits un-aided, in which case thinning may give you monster fruits.

Varieties

Choice must always be personal – local varieties, preferably – but do avoid the commonest mistakes: 'Cox's Orange Pippin' is not easy to grow or crop well; 'Bramley's Seedlings' get too big and are everywhere; 'James Grieve' is good only when fresh off the tree, as are most old earlies; 'Beauty of Bath' and 'Worcester Pearmain' are heirlooms that should be grown only in the largest collections. Do have at least one russet and a good cooker such as 'Rev. W. Wilks', 'Newton Wonder' or 'Norfolk Beauty'. 'Blenheim Orange' and 'Laxton's Superb' store well into the New Year, 'Ribston Pippin' and 'Brownlees Russet' till past Easter. 'Granny Smith' is a hard green apple that hangs on the tree well into the New Year and stores very well – I have found edible apples under the tree in April

TOP These needed more thinning especially as the leaf area is poor.
BOTTOM These could have been thinned better as they're congested as they swell.

(hidden among some lavender where the birds had not spotted them). 'Sturmer Pippin' is a long keeper more suited to milder damper areas, and 'D'Arcy Spice' a long keeper for the drier, colder regions. 'Court Pendu Plat' is a very old yellow-fleshed variety well suited to difficult sites – high up, or with heavy soils, or with late frosts – where a very long-storing dessert is required as it will keep well into May. Grow it with the tough late-flowering 'Crawley Beauty' to pollinate it; this cooker can be eaten and keeps till the end of February.

Harvest

The earlies need to be picked and dried, puréed or juiced before they go pappy – which is within hours of picking. They often give a soft flabby white dried ring, and a whitish juice that is quite sharp, even though sweet. The midseasons can be picked as they start to fall and again processed as soon as possible. It is the lates that are hard to judge: generally, if they are falling you had better gather them, but the longer they stay on the tree the better – except that bird and weather damage will intensify day by day, so you have to take a decision. I harvest the lates in three shots anyway, so spreading the risk and leaving some till the frosts if I have a general surplus in store.

Go back and re-read everything written about picking gently, spreading the grip with the palm, lifting the fruit away with the small stalk – pedicel – intact, laying each fruit in a padded tray or whatever and then gently taking them to the store without bumping them. The fruits are best left with the store at first open at night so they can sweat and breathe, then closed up after a week or so.

Before picking, collect up existing windfalls and select those worth processing on the one hand, and those for disposal as infested or infected on the other; then leave the rest in a ring around (but not touching) the trunk, to fob off the birds and wasps but also so they will not have to be checked again. Then pick: select the best for storage; put the second-best aside for processing soon; and put any infested, infected or dropped with the windfalls to be processed straight away.

Preserving and use

Apples used to be coated with a solution of sodium bicarbonate, which, once dried, left a fungicidal powdery coating that helped them keep. They were also individually wrapped; I pack mine in layers of shredded newspaper. They can be layered in big buckets, but are best on trays. Their ideal storage temperature is cool but never frosty; most homes are too warm and dry, so if a proper or bodged store cannot be made, keep them in a rodent-proof shed or unheated garage. They will pick up taints from smelly things, so be careful what you keep them with. And, of course, label them, with their names and the months best for using: some are woody when eaten too early, and after their time they go pappy or soft inside, wither and decay. Do not let this happen; convert about-to-go-over stored apples into purée and freeze that – by now, space will be available, believe me.

Apples dry really well, easily; all you need do is peel and core them and then slice and hang the rings, finger thickness, on strings or clean canes, or lay them on wire trays. The rings can be dipped in lemon juice or salt or sugar water before drying to stop them browning. The earlies make softer, pappier, whiter rings than later croppers, the russets dry well and cookers can dry as well as dessert apples.

To peel quantities of apples

First wash them, then follow the steps below, doing all the apples in the batch one step at a time, and returning the apples between steps to water – with added salt if they are varieties that turn brown quickly.

1 Cut the top and bottom off thinly.

2 Core – I use a sharpened wide tube, and afterwards push the core out with a wooden spoon handle. If you peel before coring, the fruit may burst; if you core before removing the ends, it's harder and messier to push the skins through the corer top and bottom than it is peeled flesh.

3 Peel around continuously with a sharp knife, or up and down with a peeler. Finally slice all the apples into rings, or whatever. All the parings and cores (as long as bruised and mouldy or pesty bits were removed with their underlying parts as you worked) can be juiced, or boiled down and the purée sieved out for other uses.

The most valuable of apple products is the juice, which is refreshing drunk, freezes well and can be used to improve countless jams, jellies and juices. However, second to this is the purée, which is a dessert in its own right, also freezes well, makes thin jams thick, can be used to make chutneys, pickles and curries galore, and is the basis for the whole range of fruit leathers made from other fruits, such as strawberries, that have good flavour but little bulk. When storing, it is worth noting on your packaging whether different batches of purée are sweeter, smoother or more acid, and thus suitable for different uses.

Some apples turn to a froth naturally as you heat them; others

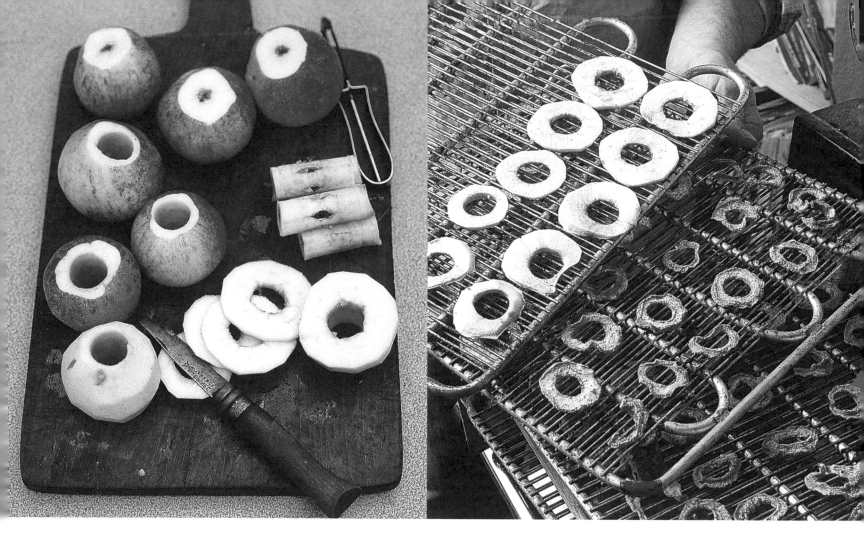

ABOVE LEFT **The stages of apple ring preparation: coring, peeling slicing.**
ABOVE RIGHT **Apple rings drying.**

have to be mechanically sieved to break them down. If you want lots of creamy apple sauces, you'll find most cookers ideal: 'Howgate Wonder', 'Norfolk Beauty', 'Ontario', 'Bramley's Seedling' and especially 'George Neal' will cook to froths rather than staying firm. If you want slices that remain firm for tarts, pies or bottling, you'll find most dessert varieties will do this, or alternatively firm cookers are 'Cox's Pomona' and 'Lane's Prince Albert'. For baking you want a tasty creamy flesh that stays firm in the bursting skin, so 'Lord Suffield', 'Lord Derby' and 'Rev. W. Wilks' are good choices.

I've tried smoking dried apple rings to see whether they would go well with cheese and in quiches and bread – it worked, but I don't reckon they'll catch on.

If dried rings are to be reconstituted, use cold water overnight; if you use the juice it can make the rings tougher – though they can be poached in juice, or the concentrate, once rehydrated.

Given a glut of apples, which is not unusual, a sensible approach is to dry some but juice the bulk, and to freeze the tastiest, brightest juice for drinking later and concentrate the rest down to freeze for adding to jams and so on – or turn the spare juice into cider (see pages 66–67). If the washed apples were well prepared and all the rotten bits rejected, the pulp after squeezing for the juice can be further processed. You can slowly cook it down and extract a good purée, which is excellent for setting jams with all the seed and skin extracts, or for leathers. Or you can break up the squeezed pulp (freezing helps soften the lumps further), cover it with juice and ferment it in a tub with a white-wine yeast. (Make a generous starter and mix it in well with the pulp.) Once partly fermented, the pulp needs to be strained through a fine cloth filter into glass demijohns or a barrel, and the wine finished as normal. This makes a weak apple wine, with quite a pronounced almond taste from the seeds; if you want it to keep, you need to add an extra four to eight ounces of sugar per gallon (125–250g per 5 litres) and allow it to ferment further before bottling.

Apples are not usually frozen whole; however, apple juice, its concentrate and the purée are frozen easily. The purée can also be turned into bases for curries, sauces and so on before being frozen.

Apple leather is not normally made on its own, but apple is used as the base for most fruit leathers (see page 41). My personal favourites are apple, strawberry and apricot; apple and blackcurrant; and apple and mixed fruits with lemon. Also, although leather should ideally be made from fresh apples and fruits boiled down, it can be made from the frozen items later. Even more economical – and making for a much sweeter product – is combining surplus and failed jams with apple purée to make a leather.

The fresh pressed juice can be so good that you'll need to taste each batch and freeze the best for later quaffing. Then any juice not needed for cider, or for bottling or mixing with other fruits, is best concentrated down by slow simmering. Once thick and syrupy it takes up less space when frozen, or may even be kept in the fridge (with some risk of it fermenting). The concentrate is very useful for adding to liqueurs, jellies, sauces and scrumptious sticky desserts.

Apples are not usually jammed on their own – though crab-apple jelly is a great favourite, and apple jelly can be used to carry other flavours such as mint, sage or ginger or to embalm other fruits. And the use of apple juice or concentrate to help set other jams can be carried further. Using apple purée with the other fruits or their purées can greatly increase the amount of jammy stuff produced, though it now is more like a lemon curd or a fruit cheese or butter in texture – which indeed is what it becomes. Apple and strawberry purées heated with half as much sugar as for jam produce a strawberry apple butter, which has great flavour and is easier to pile thick onto bread than the notoriously runny strawberry jam. However, it does not store as well as the jam unless frozen. Plumple is another favourite, in which plums and apple together make a more gooey spread than plums alone.

Apples are not often pickled either on their own or as chunks in other preserves, but as apple purée they are a good base for sauces for pickles, chutneys and so on, often combining well with tomato purée and onions. They are not generally made into liqueurs, but do feature heavily in mystic love potions. And undoubtedly their most famous use is for making cider (see pages 66–67). If living in a civilised country you could, of course, distil your cider to make apple brandy, but this is sadly banned in our freedom-loving UK.

plumple

Take equal amounts of both ripe plums and cooking apples or under-ripe dessert apples. De-stone the plums and cut into four or more pieces. Peel and core the apples and cut into slices. Place into a pan, just cover with water and cook until soft. Alternatively, simply chop all the fruit roughly, cover with water and simmer till soft enough to sieve out the stones, pips and so on. In either approach, weigh the purée and add the same amount of white sugar to the pan and simmer gently, stirring constantly until the sugar has dissolved. Turn up the heat until it nearly boils and the purée turns 'jammy', take off the heat and pour into hot, sterilised jars. You could add a little lemon zest along with the sugar for an extra tang.

baked apples

For firm baked apples choose large eating varieties, as most cookers will turn into a purée. Take four to six apples; core and peel them (the peel can be left on if so liked). If peeled, rub them over with butter. Using the corer, take 'clean cores' from another apple and insert these pieces into the base of the hole where the core was in each of your baking apples. Stuff the apples with a mixture of dried fruit and brown sugar. Add a small knob of butter on top. Bake in the oven, 180°C/350°F/gas mark 4, for about half an hour until they brown on top. Serve with custard or ice cream.

For firm baked apples choose large eating varieties, as most cookers will turn into a purée

Pears *(Pyrus communis)*

Pears are a wonderful fruit fresh for dessert; keep an eye on them till the smell improves, and (for most) the skin turns yellow, as they ripen. Much more than apples, they need to be eaten at the right time. They would have been perfect today, were woody yesterday and will be gone over tomorrow. They are not difficult to grow – but are difficult to grow really well. They need more warmth than apples, and a free-draining soil that is always moist but never wet. Yet they can even crop – late – on a wall in cool shade.

There are good dwarf stocks for pears, and even more than with apples it is advisable to have cordon or espalier trained trees, as the cropping of bush trees or standards is just too much to handle. The choicest pears deserve a warm wall if you want magnificent fruits. Pears can be moved more easily at any age than most fruit trees, as the dwarfing stocks have a compact fibrous root system; this also means they can be grown in big tubs if you water them religiously. There are even very dwarf patio-table pear trees that you can grow in pots, with small to average-size fruits, though for flavour I'd recommend by far the classic varieties instead.

Although apples may bruise when they drop, pears are riper when they fall, and bruise far worse, and should have been picked already. Also, although it is allowable to grass under big pear trees they still resent it, and trained trees on weak stocks do best on bare soil – or failing that a mulch. This means that fallen fruits get dirtier, and as they rot more quickly than apples, they need more frequent picking and processing. Pollination is trickier than with apples, as fewer pears are about, but several varieties such as 'Conference', 'Dr Jules Guyot' and 'Concorde' are self-fortile.

Varieties

The earlier pears ripen in August; the later ones are far better-flavoured, with the finest ripening after the frosts until midwinter. 'Jargonelle' is the best early in my book. Soon afterwards you get the much better 'Clapp's Favourite', 'Souvenir de Congrès' and 'Bartlett' ('Williams' Bon Chrétien') – which is not only a good eater but the best pear to bottle, the second-best being 'Conference'. Then the frosts bring the best of all, which must be securely indoors by this time: 'Beurre Hardy', 'Doyenne du Comice' and 'Seckle'. These last two are the very finest pears when well grown on a warm wall. Very late storing pears give less choice than with apples, with the rock-hard 'Catillac' being commonly suggested, though it is only for cooking and better for pickling. 'Winter Nelis' and 'Passe Crassane' are much better either eating or cooking. 'Glou Morceau' and 'Josephin de Malines' will keep till the New Year. Two longest-storers are the uncommon Easter 'Beurre' ('Doyenne d'Hiver') and 'Olivier de Serres'.

Harvest

Pears need to be picked sooner than apples; if they start to fall, most will soon be softening and browning in the middle as they go 'sleepy'. As with apples, you need to pick them over several times, gently cupping and lifting each fruit and taking only those that come away happily. These must be handled like eggs and placed in single layers on padded trays and removed to the store. Pears can be kept chilled, like apples, but not for so long, and then they need ripening in a warm humid place; the bathroom or kitchen is probably as near as you will get without making a special ripener. Traditionally, pears were ripened in the warm humid roof space above the animals in their stables. It is not easy to ripen pears well, so expect many failures: many will wither, rot or go soft in the middle unless you are careful and lucky.

OPPOSITE **This seedling pear of my own raising stores well till late spring.**
BELOW **Pears regularly glut and their uses are few. I make a delicious and useful pear concentrate (see page 84).**

Preserving and use

Drying pears is not as easy as drying apples, as taken too soon they are woody and, too late, they are already going soft and over. They also need different treatment so as not to waste their flesh. Instead of making rings you should (usually) peel them, halve them, cut out the core and central fibres with a sharp teaspoon, and then dry (or preserve) the two halves; this saves the flesh at the top which would be lost with an apple corer. (I, however, do use a corer, as I convert all the parings and cores into pear juice by gently heating them.) Most dried pears are waxier and stickier than apples. One, the Asian or Nashi pear, is far superior as a dried fruit than fresh. Shaped like an apple, you should peel and core it like an apple. The texture after drying is almost sultana- or raisin-like, very sweet and far nicer than the gritty, oddly perfumed fresh flesh.

Pear purée can be combined with other fruits and made into leather, but is not as effective as apple purée and better mixed with it and other fruits; not all combinations work as the pear flavour can be strong, but apricot and raspberry go very well. Pears are not generally frozen, as they turn black – but their juice and its concentrate may be. Pear sorbet is not wonderful, however, cinnamon baked pears can be frozen for later use, as can pear tarts.

Bottling pears is traditional. Any dessert pears can be bottled just as they yellow and ripen; 'Bartlett' ('Williams Bon Crétien) is probably the best variety for this. Pack the cored peeled halves in syrup made with fifty-fifty pear juice and whitecurrant/lemon juice or verjuice and four ounces of sugar per pint (100g per 600ml), then heat to boiling point for ten minutes and seal. Some would add spices – but then we are almost at pickled pears. Cooking pears need to be simmered in the syrup mix for longer, until they go soft, and can then be boiled and sealed: they will be dark but don't worry.

Pears are hard to juice. Before they ripen and soften they are woody and not very sweet; then they ripen and immediately soften further and go brown inside; and the next day they are rotting. If you crush and press them like apples, you get hardly any juice but toothpaste-like extrusions of pear paste everywhere. A better way of juicing pears is to heat them gently. Although this method works for many fruits and vegetables, long, slow heating destroys too many of the nutrients to be used where other alternatives exist. But for pears it is the only real option. What is more, it can be done when they're a tad unripe all the way to well softened up and browning, as long as they have not actually fermented or rotted. It is a very handy way of using up all the peelings and bits left over from preparing pears for other purposes. Put all the chopped bits in a big, deep, covered pan and gently heat it up; overnight they become a

small quantity of bits floating in a lot of clear juice, which can be strained off and bottled or frozen. Or it can be slowly boiled down to a pear concentrate, which can be frozen or kept in the fridge. Pear concentrate is less acid than apple concentrate, yummier, more like maple syrup and so easy to use in desserts, cereals and so on.

Pears are rarely jammed or jellied, although they could be; likewise they are not often turned into cheeses and butters – although they can be, in which case they need more spices than apple. And I've never crystallised or candied them, which would be quite easy… in fact, thinking about it now, I might do some.

Pears are great pickled. Peel and core them, cut into quarters or smaller, then simmer in spices and vinegar with sugar mixed in at about two pounds to a pint (900g to 600ml), making sure the liquid covers them. Once they're soft, drain and pack them into jars; then boil the vinegar till it's syrupy thick and pour it over them, covering them deep, and seal the jars. Bits of pickled pear can also be used in mixed pickles, brown sauces and especially in chutneys.

Pears, of course, make perry; however, it is most important to use perry pears for a palatable product. Pear brandy can be made, where legal, from perry; traditionally, this is then put in a bottle with a ripe pear in it. To do this, hang the bottle on the tree, poking a still tiny fruitlet through the neck on a long stem into the bottle, and allow it to ripen there. Detach it, carefully wash both pear and bottle, pour in your spirit and amaze your friends. The pear will keep for a long time. Pears have not yet featured in my liqueur selections, though as I'm now contemplating candying and crystallising some I might make a cinnamon baked-pear liqueur to go with them.

cinnamon baked pears

If the pears are large, prepare them as for baked apples, but if they are small, peel, halve and core them. Mix together five parts caster sugar, two parts powdered cinnamon (for example, if you have about six large pears use 2¹/₂oz/60g sugar with a tablespoon cinnamon), a pinch of allspice, a hint of freshly grated nutmeg and ground ginger, and a tad of salt. Place the pears into an ovenproof dish; rub them all over with softened butter and the spiced sugar. Bake in a hot oven, 200°C/400°F/gas mark 7, until softened and caramelised on top.

The same spices go well with stewed pears, and peppercorns or cloves can add extra warmth

OPPOSITE Pick pears early rather than late.
RIGHT Stewing pears is a great way to preserve them.

Quinces (*Cydonia oblonga*)

Quinces are of two sorts: the usually red-flowered Japanese more ornamental shrubby Chaenomeles form, and the small tree-like Cydonia form. The former is easy to fit against any convenient wall, or scrambling for space as a free-standing shrub. This plant is hard to train neatly, but fruits almost without fail. The Cydonia is more like a pear in both tree and fruit, needing a warm site with a moist soil to crop well with their bigger, more aromatic fruits.

Quinces should be picked just as they fall, and both sorts can be stored for some time, as with pears; in fact one of their odd uses is as room-perfumers, as their strong sweet smell is most pervasive. Either fruit can be hard enough to knock nails in with; the roughly chopped fruits are best boiled, sieved and made into their fine clear jelly, which is excellent. They can be boiled, sliced and bottled, or stewed with other fruits, and their purée can be added to leathers – and I guess quinces could be candied. Their cheese is 'Dulce de Membrillo'. Slices, if you can make them (chunks is more realistic) of the larger quinces added to apple pies and tarts hold their texture and add extra aromatic flavour.

Medlars (*Mespilus germanica*)

These odd fruits are worth noting as some people really like them; personally I find a rotten pear remarkably similar. Anyway, to put my bias aside, these resemble, and are closely related to, small pears crossed with giant rosehips. After picking they are stood in a frost-free place till they blet (ripen to the point of rotting) or soften, when the pulp is extracted and made into a jam or confections with cream and liqueurs. Please try this before you invest in a tree. The trees are small and quite attractive, with huge flowers like apple blossom and a contorted frame that looks great in winter against the sky. Medlars can be grown where a small pear or quince might not prosper, if you really want one.

STONE FRUITS

These are most successful in warmer, drier regions; far fewer varieties can be grown in milder, damper areas – especially where they do not get a cold winter, as they have strong dormancy requirements. They all like rich soils well mulched and with lime in them; they may not crop well without it. They also all suffer from frosts taking off their flowers and small fruitlets, and most, save the plums, are worth growing in tubs and moving under cover from midwinter till after harvest. Prone to gluts, the fruits do not keep well and must be promptly processed.

Plums and gages (*Prunus domestica, Prunus italica*)

Plums, including the even tastier but similar gages, are delicious fruits. They come in yellows and greens, reds and purples, even blacks and blues, with green or yellow flesh and stones that either are hard to remove, or just drop out. Plums tend to be more acid than gages – so if it's jam and preserves you're after, do the plums, and eat your gages for dessert.

Not only do plums and gages have a wide range of flavours, but this can be made more pronounced if you skin some varieties – especially the dark ones – before jamming or juicing. You get a totally different jam or juice with and without the skin, and by adding the surplus skins to another usual skin-on batch you can produce an even stronger-tasting one. These fruits do not last long or store fresh very well, though the best can be kept in good condition for some weeks if removed on their stems and suspended in a cool, dark place.

Plums as yet do not have as many dwarfing rootstocks as other fruits, and are harder to train. So they are almost invariably grown as bushy trees, which mostly get too big even on so-called dwarfing stocks, so if you want to grow several varieties, you need a lot of space. Several crop happily – if late and less sweetly – on a sunless north wall, though. If they are to go on a wall, get the most recent dwarfing stock and shape it like a herring fishbone: one main stem with lots of small branches coming off it, all flat against the wall.

Fortunately, many plums are self-fertile – though they nearly always do better with a partner; you can have just two if they are the right couple. Unfortunately, plums really do not do very well in big tubs, being short-lived and miserable; I have found they still throw a few fruits, however, so this is about the only way of having plums in very small gardens. Plums like it even less if you bring them under cover to force them; it does work, but the returns for your efforts are small. Grown as normal, outdoors, plums tend to come in great gluts every so often when their flowers miss late frosts. As the heavy crop swells, they may break their branches! Heavy pruning with shears and props is needed, and then be ready for that glut as the window for picking is short – and wasp-strewn.

Plums like a rich, moist soil with some lime in it, and some like a warm spot, but they are not difficult other than because of their size, and the problem of late frosts taking off the early flowers. Unless trained, they are best unpruned, except remedially, and then only in summer save for first aid.

OPPOSITE **Peaches and apricots are easily forced under cover for earlier crops.**

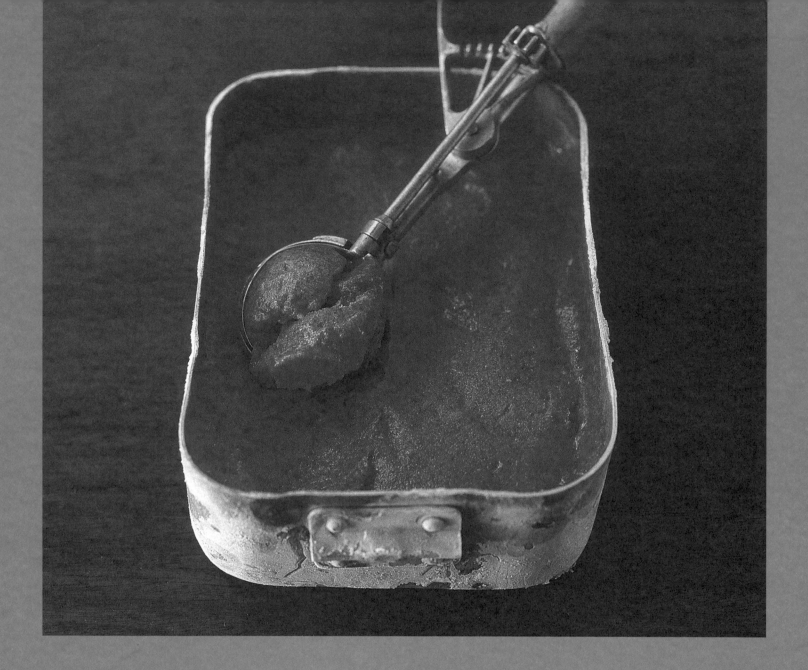

plum sorbet

Take ripe plums, clean and cut into pieces and stew with enough water to cover them until soft. Cool and sieve to remove stones and skins. Mix with an equal volume of concentrated apple juice or sugar syrup. Cool slightly then pour into an ice-cream maker and churn until frozen. Alternatively, if you don't have a machine place into a metal tub and part freeze. Whisk the mix every $1^{1}/_{2}$ hours or so to aerate and prevent ice crystals forming until you have a soft sorbet. Return to the freezer until ready to eat. If not used within weeks, the sorbet will slowly turn hard and white – this is a crystallisation and the icy mixture formed is another frozen delight.

Plum juice and sugar makes a good syrup for pouring over ice cream

Varieties

The earliest fruiters ripen in July, with such varieties as 'Early Laxton', which is multipurpose, and 'River's Early Prolific', the earliest good cooker; but the more choice varieties, such as 'Cambridge Gage' and the popular cooker 'Csar', come in August; the tasty dual-purpose 'Marjorie's Seedling' and the ubiquitous (because it is good) 'Victoria' ripens in September; and then the divine 'Coe's Golden Drop' and the large dessert 'Severn Cross', and late cookers such as the old central 'European Quetsche', finish the season in October. For prunes, grow 'Giant Prune' ('Burbanks'), which ripens in early September and is a good all-round pollinator. Look for purple-leaved ornamental plums going for the asking, as these often set good crops of dark fruits which make excellent jam – something few people realise.

Harvest

The first plums to ripen may have plum moth maggots, so be observant, pick them up and dispose of them; any damaged plums can be cleaned if needed as there is little taint. Dessert plums can often be better eating once they're peeled, from the stalk end; it's the skins that have the dire effects. For bottling, a tad under-ripe is best – and this is certainly the case for jam, where you need less-than-ripe plums to keep the flavour acid enough; otherwise add white- or redcurrant juice. For drying, the longer they can be left on the tree without becoming damaged, the better. Plums do not hang long, but they do ripen unevenly, so pick carefully. Many of the gages become translucent when ripe. Shaking down plums may be safer from tall trees and where wasps are a problem.

Preserving and use

Plums dry well – very well: unfortunately they all turn into prunes sooner or later. Initially, though, the different plums dry differently, even retaining some colour, but they continue to darken relentlessly, sometimes exuding a farina of sugar. Drying is simple enough: halve and stone the plums and dry them on wire trays, slowly so they don't darken too much. To speed up the processing, make a stone-gripper: take a typical plum stone, hammer it gently into the end of a hand's-width length of copper tube; do this consecutively with several stones until the mouth of the tube has been moulded such that a stone fits almost halfway in. Then get a bamboo cane a tad longer to fit snugly inside the tube. Now halve each plum round the middle and twist; one half comes free and the stone remains in the other half. Push the pipe over the stone, twist – and the stone will come out stuck in the tube; then push the stone out of the tube from the other end using the bamboo cane. As with coring batches of apples, it is quicker to cut them all, halve them all, and twist the stones out of all of them as a batch.

Plums can be reduced to a tasty leather, for which they are best mixed with apple; their flavour overwhelms other fruits.

Plums can be frozen whole, but the stones give a taint of cyanide's almondy bitterness so are best removed beforehand; then freeze the plums open on trays and repack them in bags or boxes. They can be reduced to a purée and frozen or made into very tasty sorbets and ices. For some reason, purple and red plums are usually preferred to yellow for freezing, bottling and chutneys.

To bottle plums (again, red or purple preferably), pick them just under ripe and on the smaller size, pack in wide-mouthed bottles, cover with hot plum juice, surround with warm water and heat for half an hour till the water is simmering; then hold it there for ten minutes or so, seal and cool. Plums are hard to squeeze juice out of, and most kitchen juicers waste too much, so they may be better heated slowly in a covered pan. Start them off with just a little water or juice, and once the fruits have broken down, strain off the

BELOW **Plums in rum – yum.**

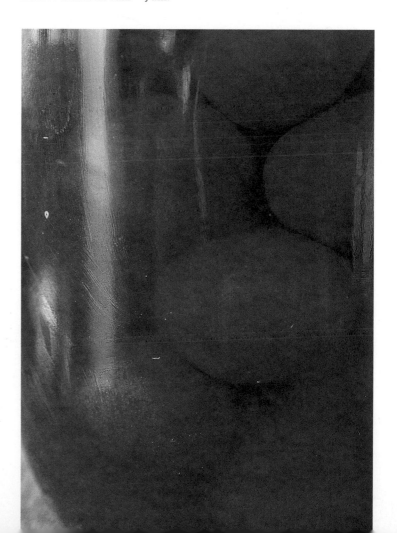

liquid, which can be bottled or frozen. The pulp can go for leather.

Plums and gages make great jams, which usually set easily. You can remove the stones before boiling the fruit down, fudge them out as the fruit breaks down or strain them out before the sugar goes in – as usual roughly fifty–fifty sugar to pulp. Plums are harder to make into a clear jelly, but easy to turn to thick mixed-fruit jams with apple purée. Plum juice and sugar makes a good syrup for pouring over ice cream. Plums make richly flavoured preserves, cheeses and butters. Sugared plums are a favourite; they candy or crystallise easily and their strong colours and flavours make them good for this.

Pickling plums is traditional – usually whole small dark ones. Prick them all over with a pin, soak for a day in vinegar, bring to a simmer with the spices till soft and then bottle them. Plums add a lot of sweetness and body to chutneys and pickle sauces, and plum sauce was once as popular as tomato ketchup is now. Plums are salted and brined as delicacies in Japan; these have failed to please my tastes but the idea offers more possibilities.

Plums make excellent wines, if a bit prone to cloudiness and easily gaining off flavours if made too strong. The distilled brandy is better. Possibly, though, it is in the liqueurs made after the manner of sloe gin that plums excel; these capture the flavours best and make delightfully coloured drinks full of summer goodness.

Damsons (Prunus damascena)

Damsons are small black-blue plums, less sweet and with a stronger spicier flavour. The trees are tougher, bushier and not huge, so good in hedges and as windbreaks. They are okay as a jam, though often need extra water or juice or they may set very thick; as for damson jelly, I've never tried making it as I like the skins. Damsons are traditionally turned into cheeses and butters and are often accompaniments to savoury dishes. The wine, like plum, tends to haziness and off flavours but the liqueur – oh, it's wonderful, one of the best, with dark rum and brown sugar.

Bullaces, mirabelles et al. (Prunus institia)

Acidic little wild yellow or blue-black plums, but not sloes, these may be found in huge quantities. I love the jams because of their tartness; the fruits are worth freezing to replace apricots in some dishes; the wine is obvious but has an overpowering headiness – and their liqueur is much the better. The more spherical myrobalan or cherry plum is very bland and best used as pulp for leather, or for bulking other more flavoursome jams such as apricot. True sloes do make a good liqueur, traditionally with gin, and I sometimes make sloe jelly with apple concentrate (it's useful if you're constipated!).

Apricots (Prunus armeniaca)

These are one of the choicest fruits, and the newer varieties should make them even easier to crop. They are very like plums and may crop heavily in good years; grab every fruit and use it, for they are supreme for jam, or frozen fresh or as purée. Plant them as bushes in the warmest, sunniest well-drained spots with plenty of lime – and pray. They can be trained on walls as fans relatively easily for earlier crops, and are good in tubs. They fruit even earlier – though not quite so tastily – and are very decorative and easy if you force them, by bringing their tubs under cover in late winter before the flowers open, when they will need hand pollination. Do not overfeed or over-water apricots in tubs – and water very sparingly as the fruits ripen! Outdoors, the only common problem is the frosts taking off the flowers or fruitlets; the usual measures apply. Pruning is, as for apples, though done only in summer. Outdoors, hand pollination helps, as although apricots are self-fertile there are few insects about at that time of year. I know we should thin them, but I can barely ever do any and I doubt you will either – and although benefiting from thinning, apricots may still crop really well without it.

BELOW LEFT **Flowers under cover need pollinating with a wee paintbrush or nought will happen.**
BELOW RIGHT **A forced apricot under cover can ripen a month or more ahead of outdoors.**

apricot jam

Take equal quantities of fully ripe and under ripe apricots, wash, de-stone and cut into pieces. (The stones can be shelled and the kernels used to make biscuits.) Place the apricots into a pan with the same quantity of preserving sugar, cover and leave to stand overnight so that the sugar dissolves. Next day transfer to a heavy pan and boil rapidly for 7–8 minutes until thick and 'jammy'. Stand for 10 minutes then decant into hot, sterilised jam jars. If the stones are difficult to remove, simply slit the flesh of each fruit before mixing with the sugar. During boiling, the stones will float to the surface and can be removed with a slotted spoon.

apricot christmas pudding

Take a jar and a half (about 1¹⁄₄oz/560g) of apricot jam and empty it into a bowl. Add the same volume of dried fruits, a mix of raisins, sultanas and chopped apricots, and about quarter of the jar (3oz/75g) of fine breadcrumbs. Mix in an ounce and a half (40g) of butter, 2 lightly whisked eggs and a large pinch of both powdered ginger and cinnamon and a good grating of nutmeg. Grease a 1-pint pudding basin with butter and spoon the mix in. Cover with a double layer of pleated greaseproof paper and foil and secure tightly with string around the edge of the basin. Place in a pan using a saucer as a trivet and fill a third of the way up with boiling water. Steam for 2 hours, keeping an eye on the water level at regular intervals. To serve, tip onto a hot plate, cover with hot brandy and set fire to it carefully at the table.

fruity up and down pancake

First make a pancake mix; sieve 2 ounces (60g) plain flour into a bowl. Mix together an egg with a yolk and half a pint (300ml) milk, a tablespoon of sunflower oil and a dash of vanilla extract. Make a well in the centre of the flour and add the liquid, gradually incorporating the dry ingredients until you have a smooth batter. Leave to stand for 20 minutes.

For the filling, choose any fruit in season you fancy, or have in abundance, about three-quarters of a pound (350g) in total. Soften in butter with a little sugar to taste. Heat a non-stick pan with a little oil until smoking hot. Pour about half the pancake mix in and then dot spoonfuls of the fruit all around. Now the base is set, turn down the heat and carefully pour over the rest of the mix. Cook for a minute or two, dredge with caster sugar then place under a grill to finish cooking the top. It is ready when deep golden brown. Tilt the pan to check there are no runny bits. Serve immediately with ice cream or custard.

For the filling choose any fruit in season you fancy, or have in abundance, I chose peaches, plums and raspberries

Varieties

'Alfred', 'Tomcot' and 'Goldcot' are often ripe in early July, especially on a wall; 'Moorpark' is easy to find and crops in July/August on a wall, or later off it – a tad later than 'Farmingdale', which is huge and good for freezing. Without doubt the later-ripening old 'Roman Bredase' is a must, as it is the tastiest for jam. The new varieties 'Flavourcot', 'Delicot', 'Lilicot' and so on show great promise. I have grown the 'Hunza' (the fruits are sold as dried apricots in health shops), which takes ten years to fruit but then has small white fruits in profusion; they are prone to rot but are delicious and make phenomenal jam.

Harvest

Apricots should be thinned early and often, as the young green fruits make excellent tarts. Then they need watching, as the fruits drop and go pappy once ripe. Once overripe, some hang on the trees and part-dry, but if any damp is about they will mummify.

Preserving and use

Apricots dry really well simply halved and de-stoned, and they stay tasty; they don't retain the glorious orange of the bleached commercial ones but turn a browny orange – still delicious, though. They freeze very well, and their sorbets and ices are The Best. They are easiest to de-skin as they defrost.

Apricots also bottle well, just like plums, but their drier nature makes them harder to juice, so it is better to preserve them as purée or jam: apricots make one of the best jams; take care not to heat it too quickly or it will darken. Pieces or halves of apricot are grand preserved in their jam, and apricots can be turned into wonderful cheeses and butters, with apple purée – but nothing else, as the apricot flavour is soon overwhelmed. I've not crystallised or candied them, though they should be easy; pick them earlier than for drying as they can get a tad more fibrous than plums or peaches as they ripen up.

Apricots can be pickled, they can be used for a chutney similar to – but better than – mango, and they make delicious sweet sauces. I've not heard of salting apricots, but I imagine someone somewhere does it. And I can't imagine having enough surplus to make the wine, which would probably not be brilliant. However, apricots do make delightful liqueurs, and the soaked fruits are gorgeous in place of plums as the base for Christmas pudding, making it a golden-brown sticky goo. The seeds in apricot stones are edible, unlike peach or plum stones, and make fantastic macaroon biscuits if you can amass enough.

ABOVE **Two peaches (the flat Peento here) should not be left as they will squash each other, so thin them straight away!**

Peaches (*Prunus persica*)

These are surprisingly easy to crop as bush trees in the warmer regions; their main reason for not cropping is late frosts taking off the flowers. They are not impossible to train on walls, but it is a lot of continual work. Far better to have bushes in the open in a sheltered spot, such as in front of a wall (not on it), and a warm, light, limey soil is best. Peaches do not remain productive long and are often past it after two decades. In large tubs they can be moved under cover in midwinter; this keeps them dry and avoids their leaf-curling disease, which must otherwise be treated with Bordeaux (mixture, not wine!) as the buds open. Self-fertile, they will need hand pollination under cover, and regular liquid feeding when grown in tubs.

After cropping they must go outdoors to harden up, and be brought in earlier than most other forced fruits. Peaches overcrop as of right, and really must be ruthlessly thinned so that no two fruits will touch when they're full size; leave only a sensible number per tree or you will be processing masses of under-ripe squits. Too many exhaust the tree, fail to reach any size or even ripen. Literally decimate them down to the best one in every ten; leave those and they will get huge!

Of all tree crops, peaches are the most annoying for processing as they are so sweet yet watery and their flavour ephemeral and too easily lost. A glut of peaches is very, very quickly gone to waste, and there is little you can do with them that is really worth doing a lot of. So grow them in tubs to give a longer season of small harvests rather than having one big one in the ground, and bring them under cover sequentially to extend the times of ripening. Peach pruning means one of two things: either leave the plant alone entirely as a bush, or else prune really hard, in summer, shortening all shoots back except frame extensions and strong growths replacing whole branches. Plant them in tubs and little is needed.

Varieties

Peaches are either clingstone – which are annoyingly the better – or more usefully freestone, where it is easier to get the stone out for processing. 'Peregrine', white-fleshed, and 'Rochester', yellow-fleshed, which both ripen in August, are the only two I'd recommend outdoors for a climate such as in the southern UK, and they will need to be in a very warm place anywhere further north or not so mild. The yellow-fleshed 'Rochester' preserves better than the white-fleshed 'Peregrine'. Late varieties often fail to ripen unless taken under cover, where almost all varieties do better – although the best-flavoured grow outdoors. The flattened-doughnut-shaped peento Chinese peaches, such as 'Saturn', are especially good in tubs moved under cover.

Nectarines are peach varieties with smooth skins; the two are sometimes found as sports on each other's trees. They have a higher warmth-and-light requirement and so rarely crop outdoors unless on a hot wall, and are best in tubs moved in and out. 'Lord Napier' is an old early, ripening in August.

Harvest

The only way to enjoy a peach is when it is sun-warmed, caught as it drops off the tree, peeled and eaten when you're naked – or wearing a bib, as ripe peaches are balloons full of nectar. They can be picked earlier to ripen (after a fashion) indoors over a day or two, but they'll rot as soon as you look at them. Few crops go over faster, so pick them twice daily and process immediately. Be even more careful than usual not to squeeze, bruise or bump them, as fully ripe they go off faster than hand grenades.

Preserving and use

Peaches are easy to dry, as long as you have a good warm draught to desiccate them before they mould, and they do not darken as much as plums or apricots; their flavour rather evaporates, though, so dried peaches are nowhere near as tasty as fresh. Likewise, when they're turned into leathers with apples, the taste is a bit bland; leathered on their own they have a good flavour, though it's more plum-like than the fresh. Freezing is easy (and if they are not already skinned, it's easy to do them as they defrost) – but again, little of the fresh flavour is retained and the texture is poor. Peaches keep more flavour if turned into sweetened purées, sorbets and ice creams.

Peaches are best carefully bottled, indeed the product is so different from fresh it is worth having. Dip fresh-picked, ever-so-slightly under-ripe, ideally yellow-fleshed peaches in boiling water for a half-minute or so, then in cold, and slip the skins off. Cut them in half and remove the stone, then pack in bottles and cover with hot sugar syrup or peach juice (any other flavour will overwhelm), heat immediately, very slowly, for half an hour, and then, once the water reaches simmering point, give them twenty minutes extra.

Peaches are very juicy, but the juice is thick and it goes off really fast; the fruits are best frozen or bottled as sweetened purée rather than as juice. Freezing and defrosting to give a strained juice does not separate enough. The cold vacuum extraction is best, as direct squeezing gives thin toothpaste-like purée, not juice. Peaches can be heated to get juice, but most of the flavour evaporates, just as it does when they are cooked for jam, which does not set easily, or for jelly, which never will; likewise their syrup can be too bland. They brown and lose their flavour once turned into preserves, cheeses and butters, though they can be used to bulk other stronger fruits. I'll not bother candying or crystallising them again.

Peaches are more use for pickling and chutneys and can be used much like mangoes, especially green. Peach wine is a bit disappointing, the liqueur is unexceptional, however peaches poached in peach brandy and syrup are a phenomenal dessert in their own right.

LEFT The harder you thin the bigger the fruits – fewer is better than too many.

Cherries (*Prunus cerasus/avium*)

A delightful fruit fresh, these have only one real problem: birds. No net or cage = no fruit. They are really two different sorts: all the sweet red and yellow cherries, eaten fresh, which are poor things preserved in almost any way at all; and the cooking, sour or Morello cherries, which are not usually eaten fresh but are superb for all sorts of processing. The former make bigger trees – do not believe the lies of so-called dwarfing rootstocks, which are but relatively dwarfing; the trees get bigger than wanted so are hard to confine on a wall or cage, they resent pruning and the fruits are hard to pick. Thus, although they are not happy in tubs (and even shorter-lived than ever), this has to be the way to grow them; they can also then be taken under cover – so fruits can be had in May! And some trees can be kept cool and shady for late crops.

Sweet cherries are not all self-fertile and need another, or a Morello, as partner. The other sort, the Morello, and its offspring are far more amenable; self-fertile, they stay smaller, are bushier and are happy being hard pruned, thus they can be put on walls for early and late crops. Although they can be grown in tubs moved in and out for even earlier and later crops, the fruits are primarily for cooking, so this may not return as much value as growing more sweet cherries.

The sweet cherries need a warm, sunny site with a fair soil and room to grow; beware: their roots come to the surface. They must be pruned only remedially, and then in summer. The Morellos can be pruned hard, again in summer, and they enjoy a richer, heavier, moister soil – and they'll even crop on a shady wall!

Varieties

Of the sweet cherries, the earliest, optimistically called 'May Duke', partly self-fertile, will crop in June – earlier if forced – and is a fair cooker and makes wonderful jam. 'Kentish Red', also self-fertile, is a good cooker ripening in early July. 'Stella', 'Summer Sun' and 'Sunburst' are new dessert varieties, self-fertile, cropping in mid-July and handy for tubs. Morello fruits later, in August/September, and is obligatory; ideally have one on a shady wall and another on a sunny wall to give a longer season.

Harvest

Watch the birdie! (Do not errantly believe any net or cage will keep all the birds out.) The sweet are best eaten as is but picked on the sprig, and carefully so the shoot tips don't get damaged. The Morellos can be left as long as possible to develop their strong rich flavour; however, pick some earlier for their higher acidity and freeze these till required to mix with the later, riper ones. Drying sweet cherries is tedious and unrewarding, drying the sour Morellos less so – but great care has to be taken to stop them shrivelling to nothing. The sweet cherry flavour gets lost, though the Morello and acid cookers make a fair leather with apple.

Preserving and use

Cherries are worth freezing; ideally de-stone them first. The sour and dark ones freeze better than the red, white or yellow dessert varieties, and all are best packed in syrup or juice, mixed with white- or redcurrant juice for the acidity. Likewise, the dark red acid varieties and Morellos make better sorbets and ices than the lighter dessert cherries. However, do freeze some sweet cherries to go in mixed-fruit compotes.

The darker cherries bottle better; however, their syrup may need white- or redcurrant juice to make it tart enough. Morellos are superb. Ideally de-stone them, but using them whole also works. Pour on the warm syrup, heat slowly for half an hour to a simmer, and give just ten minutes extra before sealing and cooling.

Most dessert cherries do not make good jam, being low in pectin and so hard to set – and the jelly has no hope. It is better to

cherry apple jam

Take a concentrated apple juice (preferably an acid one, say Bramley) and add to it no more than half its weight of cleaned and stoned cherries, cut in halves. (Sweet cherries carry less flavour than Morellos which make the better jelly.) Heat gently with just enough stirring to prevent sticking until the cherries soften but before they break up. Then add the same total weight of pre-warmed sugar and return to heat until it has dissolved, raise the heat till nearly boiling and, when it becomes 'jammy', jar and seal immediately.

Cherry stones are teeth crackers so be vigilant when making their jam

make a cherry-flavoured apple jelly with semi-candied cherries in it. The dark acid and Morello cherries jam better, and they are also the only ones worth making into a syrup. Cherry cheeses and butters likewise work better – well, work only – with the cooking sour cherries. And likewise you need their strong colour and flavour for candying or crystallising, but then you do get a good product – which is best stored if you seal each in a coat of chocolate. You will not get the bright red of the glacé cherries of commerce – that is a ghastly chemical dye!

Pickling, chutneys and sauces seem alien to cherries; however, I reckon Morellos could be employed much as damsons – and might you put them in piccalilli?

As with most of the stone fruits, the wine is difficult to make without haziness or off flavours, and the sweet dessert varieties do not make a strongly flavoured liqueur but get more flavour from their stones. The darker cherries and Morellos make an excellent liqueur, and the well-soaked fruits are used in cakes and Black Forest gâteaux. The reds and light cherries are best in white rum and sugar syrup; dark rum has too strong a flavour, though it can be used with Morellos.

Cherry chocolate

Make candied cherries by stoning them and soaking in hot concentrated sugar syrup, cooling and leaving them overnight. Drain, heat the syrup until it has boiled and repeat. Do this three or four times until the pieces are chewy, then drain them well. Melt some chocolate very slowly and carefully in a bain marie or double saucepan. Pour a thin layer of chocolate into a chilled metal dish pre-lined with buttered aluminium foil and swirl it around to cover the bottom and partway up the sides and place in the freezer to chill. Melt more chocolate and stir in gently about one quarter to a third of its own weight of the candied cherries then pour the mixture into the chilled chocolate 'tray' you have made and return to the freezer to set. Once set, melt more chocolate and apply a sealing coat on top of the chilled mixture and return to the freezer. Once solid through remove the slab of chocolate, peel off the foil and cut the slab with a sharp solid knife into squares by belting the back of the knife with a mallet. Alternatively do the same with an ice cube tray to get individual chunks.

LEFT **Pick cherries with, and ideally by cutting, the sprig.**

SOFT FRUITS

The soft fruits are quicker to crop; lower, so easier to cage; smaller, so easier to have more of; and easier to correct mistakes with – especially with pruning, as they bounce back. In the wild, they grow mostly at woodlands' edge, so most can crop in some shade but are earlier and sweeter in sun. Many can be grown in tubs and moved for protected, earlier or even later crops. The varieties change faster than for trees, so it is harder always to recommend good ones.

Strawberries *(Fragaria)*

No crop is tastier or more widely liked and, although they are not light work, strawberries reward the effort. The plants must all be replaced by new ones on another bed every four years, or one quarter of them every year. Only named, healthy, robust, virus-free plants should be planted. Fortunately, just a low net on short posts is needed, making them a crop that fits into a vegetable bed, and they provide a break in the usual crop rotation.

To ensure good yields, grow strawberries in humus-rich soil, with plenty of phosphates such as bone meal, and keep them well weeded. They will crop in shade but then are less sweet, come later and may be more slug-damaged. Under cloches or plastic they are sweeter and less acid, but may cook or scorch. Dry shade under trees gives poor crops. Water their soil profligately in dry weather. Applying seaweed sprays fortnightly up until cropping improves vigour, crop and flavour. Onions and borage are good companions.

In the open, strawberries will crop from early summer. With most varieties the crop fades away, but some go on cropping or crop again in autumn until stopped by the frosts. By having early and late sorts in pots, in shady and sunny borders, by growing on ridges or up in 'raised gutters', you can extend their season by months – especially if you combine these options with using glass or plastic cover if this has sufficient ventilation. A few early fruits can be forced if you simply move plants potted in autumn under some bright airy cover.

It is technically feasible to crop strawberries all year round, but they become prone to mould and crop lightly. One major problem is that the plants are fixed as much by daylight length as by warmth, so look for the latest daylight-neutral varieties bred for forcing if you want winter crops, or control the day length with extra lighting.

Varieties

There is a huge range of usual strawberries with many different flavours, as well as varying in shape and colour, from early summer. The ever-bearing remontant and climbing varieties crop through summer and are joined by the autumn cropping varieties. All have different flavours. 'Royal Sovereign' was for years the very best, and still has a brilliant flavour but is hard to find. The 'Cambridge Vigour' and 'Cambridge Favourite' varieties have proved popular for some time too. 'Marshmello' was a recent one with good flavour; 'Gariguette' is a French one with great flavour. 'Aromel' and 'Mara des Bois' are good for autumn flavour. Then there are the Alpines, in red, white and yellow, which form little tussocks and are well worth having – and, of course, the real wild strawberry, with masses of tiny running stems and gorgeous tiny fruits is well suited to wild corners.

If any of these are grown in any sensible number and picked regularly, then after dessert use there is rarely enough left for a batch of jam – except if you store the 'seconds' till enough is

BELOW **Remember you cannot have too many strawberries – plant more now.**

available. Unfortunately this is made quicker if you mix varieties. Don't. At picking, every 'jam quality' berry should be kept to its own-variety freezer tub or bag, with only the best sent on to the table. Then, when enough have been collected, you can jam that variety alone for its unique flavour. The Alpine when fully ripe is aromatic and delicious, if most seedy – many of the seeds can be shaken off the tiny pointed fruits when they are frozen. Do try every variety you can, as the flavours vary so much, and grow loads; you cannot have too many strawberries.

Harvest

You don't have to wait – white bits on red strawberries are still edible, but redder usually means sweeter. Pick often. If you want the fruits to keep fresh longest, cut each of them off with its stalk – and when dry! And do not bruise. As you pick, carefully place the fruits into containers lined with cooling leaves or similar padding. Pick and dispose of mouldy ones immediately before the mould spreads.

BELOW **Size does not matter – it's flavour that counts.**

Preserving and use

Strawberries cannot be kept fresh for more than a few days before spoiling, and must be processed quickly. Commercially, they are dried, but most of my attempts at drying have failed. Freezing is the answer. Only a few varieties are sold as good for freezing, and those because they retain a semblance of texture after defrosting. However, any frozen strawberries are relished by children as treats, can be mixed in compotes and are tasty turned into sorbets and juices. Pick and freeze them regularly; you really can't ever have too many, and they can be turned into other goodies when you have time.

I freeze strawberries on open trays, divided into the perfect – for desserts – and the rest, which will be soon used for other purposes. Strawberries, once defrosted, turn into a clear juice, which can be mixed with sugar syrup for a tasty drink or made into a sorbet. The more solid part of the fruit left is then useful in compotes, or cooked in desserts such as sponges, or turned to a purée or jam. However, its greatest demand is to go with apple and apricot purée when it makes one of the most desirable fruit leathers of all.

Strawberry jam is one of the most popular, yet one of the most difficult to get to set, especially in a cool wet year. Use up the edible but unpalatable berries by all means: the overripe, and even a small percentage of unripe part-green fruits if they're cut small – but no rotten bits please.

Set can be improved if you first slice and sugar the fresh fruits to separate much of the juice overnight; this gives a syrup for later use and a condensed fruit mass that can be turned into a good thick jam that sets more readily. Taking away too much syrup does remove some of the flavour – but then so would boiling off that extra water! Simply adding more sugar to 'wet' fruits does not cause the jam to set! Add sugar and also apple concentrate or purée or redcurrant/whitecurrant/lemon juice or verjuice; any of these will improve the acidity and set of a strawberry jam – although will sadly also add other flavours.

Strawberries are very moist and hard to crystallise, with the small Alpines and wild ones proving least difficult. And although you can bottle them, little is to be gained by doing this rather than jamming and juicing them. They do make a pleasing sweet liqueur with rum or other alcohol, but this needs a bit of lemon or similar added or else it's insipid; likewise, strawberry wine is not as good as strawberry and gooseberry.

strawberry sponge

Wash, hull and cut in half, if large, your supply of strawberries. (You can use frozen too but defrost and drain thoroughly, reserving the juice). Cream together an equal weight of caster sugar with softened butter until light and fluffy (so if you have 7 ounces (200g) of strawberries, use the same amount of sugar and butter). Gradually add lightly whisked eggs (2 if you're using 7 ounces of stawberries), then fold in the same amount of sifted self raising flour. Add the reserved strawberry juice at this point or, if using fresh strawberries, add a splash of milk to the mix just to loosen slightly. Spoon into a greased dish or cake tin and scatter over the strawberries. Bake in a medium oven, 180°C/350°F/gas mark 4, for 40 minutes, until cooked through and springy to the touch. Cool on a wire rack.

Spoon into the dish and scatter over the strawberries

Raspberries *(Rubus idaeus)*

A wonderful delight when fresh, raspberries sadly travel badly and only the toughest sorts get sold in shops, and they're expensive – so they're well worth growing at home. And for their major use, as jam, freshness is essential for a good set. There are many new varieties, and these crop far better than most of the older sorts; self-sown seedlings are often poor croppers but may have real flavour. Old plants – over a decade old, that is – unless proving very productive are probably best replaced wholesale with new stock.

To ensure good crops, grow raspberries in moist, humus-rich soil and keep them well mulched and ruthlessly pruned. They will crop in shade but then are less sweet, come later and may be more acid and juicier. Dry shade under trees gives poor crops. Thin the canes to a hand's breadth apart, as well as pruning out all the old canes once they have cropped. Applying seaweed sprays fortnightly up until cropping improves vigour, crop and flavour. Water their soil profligately in dry weather.

Raspberries can be summer or autumn fruiting, and with several varieties it is possible to have them from early summer until hard frosts – and though those last pickings are rarely very sweet they are welcome. The same variety can be planted in both shade and sun or on either side of a wall to give up to a month's longer cropping. But raspberries do not like being grown in pots, and resent even more being under cover, and although they will survive and crop in huge containers these must be kept cool and well watered. Needless to say, no net = no fruit. The fruit-maggot problem can be avoided if you grow autumn croppers; otherwise, accept some damage and reject the damaged fruits, or remove the pests during processing.

Harvest

A row may crop over several weeks, and the picking needs to be done daily or fruits will go over. By the time you have finished a row, the first cane will have ripened another fruit or two. In order to find hiding fruits, lie down under the canes and look up – try it! Shaking helps, but gets bits in your eyes. You cannot get the whole crop in one pick, so be prepared to process each batch as it comes, or freeze each one and then process them together later. Pick the fruits carefully off the plugs, in other words pick gently, leaving the plug; if the fruit won't come easily, don't force it!

Raspberries do not keep for long if they are wet, so never pick

LEFT **Raspberries hang down, get underneath and look up to spot them.**

raspberry ripple ice cream

Defrost and drain frozen raspberries (use the pulp for something else – say leather). And to the juice add its own weight of caster sugar and warm till it has just dissolved, then chill. Take a very good-quality vanilla ice cream and place plum sized chunks in a suitable plastic container, pour over some of the syrup, then more chunks of ice cream and more syrup, pressing them all down with the spoon. Press the ice cream down firmly to remove as much air as possible and freeze. Remove from the freezer about 15 minutes before you're ready to eat.

them after rain if you can avoid it, and they rot rapidly if warm, so keep them chilled. Line trugs or baskets with cool leaves, and never allow fruits to pile deep or the bottom ones will be squashed and spoilt. If you want to keep them longest, cut the fruit stalks with scissors and do not touch the fruits.

Preserving and use
Unlike most fruits, fresh raspberries can be eaten in large quantities to little discomfort. They go well with yogurts, cream and cakes, and the classic summer pudding is usually made with more raspberries than other fruits. Their delicate flavour is overwhelmed by others, so in mixed-fruit dishes they are somewhat lost.

Raspberries can be juiced or pressed before or after freezing, though the juice is insipid unless mixed with a lot of sugar and/or redcurrant juice to bring the flavour out. I imagine raspberries could be dried, though they would be seedy things; however, with apple they make a very good fruit leather. Although I've not tried it, they strike me as a fruit that could be smoked for preservation – but with what you would eat them, and whether you would want to, I'm not sure. Raspberries are easy to freeze, open on foil

trays and bagged afterwards; they pick up taints, so make sure containers or bags are well sealed. Raspberries make among the tastiest sorbets and ices, and their delicious syrup – much better than all other berry syrups, save strawberry – is The One for layering in real vanilla ripple.

Jam and jelly are what most raspberries are grown for; both are easy to set only when the fruit is really fresh. Often raspberries are blended with redcurrant juice for bulk, and to make their jam set. The vinegar is excellent (but not as tasty as the syrup). My same reservations apply to crystallising raspberries as to drying them: their seediness is a disadvantage. Some varieties have much bigger seeds than others, making them less useful for jam and so on, but okay for jelly and for leathering. And although they tend to go to a purée, it's possible to bottle raspberries without added sugar. As they are quite low in sugar their use in wine-making is limited, but they make a delicious liqueur after the manner of sloe gin – although the flavour of raspberries is better captured in white rum. The leaves have also been used for teas, potions and syrups, especially for the latter days of pregnancy.

raspberry conserve

Pick the fresh raspberries and hurry straight to the kitchen. Wash and immediately heat them in a closed pan rapidly but gently with a swirling motion to prevent sticking and burning.

Once most of the berries have softened, but before they break down totally, add the same weight of pre-warmed caster sugar. Stir continuously while heating to boiling point and then pour into small heated jars. Seal them 1 minute after you are absolutely sure all the sugar has completely dissolved. .

Keep in the cool and use quickly once opened as this recipe is for the **stunning flavour** not keeping **quality,** and does not work as well with anything other than the **fresh picked** fruit!

Blackberries and hybrid berries – loganberries, boysenberries, tayberries et al *(Rubus spp.)*

Undoubtedly, blackberries picked in the wild may have better flavour than most garden varieties. But they may also be worse. Certainly, if you have limited space it is not sensible to grow blackberries unless wild ones are not to be had or you really adore them. The hybrid berries cannot be gathered in the wild and so have more value as garden plants. The thornless varieties are not often good choices, as their flavour and cropping are rarely as good as with thorny ones.

They all have long canes that need to be pruned out and replaced by new ones each year; they require strong posts and wires to restrain them and should be planted about five paces apart, some further – the 'Himalayan Giant' and 'Bedford Giant' both need twenty feet. The latter ripens one berry – the central or 'king' berry – in each panicle in summer ahead of all the others.

Blackberries are not very easily croppable in any reasonable-size container, though the hybrid berries may last a year or three in a big tub. They do not like being under cover, so their season is fairly restricted to summer till the frosts, although they do not all crop together, with some of the hybrids coming earlier with the raspberries.

Happy on any soil, they will give the best flavour when not overfed but well mulched and in moist – not wet – soil. Seaweed sprays and wood ashes are of benefit, of course. Although sweetest when grown in the sun, they crop in reasonable shade, and the tayberry actually does better on my light dry soil when on the shady side of a fence, there producing larger, more succulent fruits.

Blackberries are rarely appreciated much as a fresh fruit, except by some; nor are the loganberry and the boysenberry, which are better for jams. The tayberry does make a good dessert fruit, as well as good jam.

The Japanese wineberry is a species of blackberry. It has orange-red fruits that fool the birds; these are sweet and sticky and have small seeds so can be eaten in profusion. The stems are bristly with few thorns, and decoratively russet-coloured, with lime-green leaves – it's a good choice for the ornamental fruit garden. It makes an unusual jelly, reluctant to set.

The biggest problem with blackberries, other than their thorns when you're picking, is the thorns on their seeds. These harden up and are why the fruits give you gyp if you eat them late in the season, 'when the devil has spat on them'. The seeds of the hybrids more resemble raspberries and are not so fierce; even so, many prefer the jellies to the jams.

Harvest

Harvest is a dicey affair: thick jackets or old socks will protect the arms, extra trousers the legs, but the fingers must suffer as these fruits need to be gently picked to keep. Some fruits pull off the plug as with raspberries, but others bring it with them. If blackberries are to be jellied, they do not need to be as carefully picked as the hybrids intended for jam. These berries will not keep for even a few hours if they are wet or crushed. Watch out for partially dead shrivelled berries – or, worse, dead flies shrivelled and dried up on them. Some hybrids give several pickings over weeks; birds will steal the fruits unless they're protected. To keep the new canes out of your way while you pick, pull them together and away with ex-bicycle-tube elastic bands equipped with bicycle-spoke S-hooks.

Preserving and use

The finest fruits of any of these berries can be frozen for dessert or compote use, and the bulk for processing later. Blackberries are not as useful for freezing as the choicer hybrids such as the tayberry and, sadly, the Japanese wineberry is a bit insipid afterwards. The hybrids all make good frozen sorbets (which are better made with cooked juice) – much tastier than blackberry sorbet, which without apple is mawkish.

All these fruits can be bottled in their own juices, or their juice turned into syrups and squashes and then bottled or frozen. There is a big difference between the cold extracted and the cooked flavours of the juices, which all have good colours, and they are generally acid enough.

It is with jamming that these berries come into their territory. The hybrids make the most excellent full-bodied rich jams, which set reasonably well on their own and can easily be helped along with apple purée. The blackberry is better as the jelly – one of the best to sweeten with apple or pear concentrate, which gets rid of the annoying seeds – and of course the fruits are well diluted in the traditional blackberry and apple crumble (see page 106).

Any of these berries can be used in mixed preserves, or made into cheeses or leather – for which they are excellent, as they are quite substantial even after the seeds have been removed. However, because of their strong flavours, they work best on their own, or with apple. Their seedy natures mean they are not usually included in chutneys or pickles, nor crystallised. The blackberry makes a traditional wine, but I do not rate it much; the liqueur is much better and more port-like. The hybrids make interesting wines and liqueurs, each with its own distinctive flavour. The vinegar is very health-giving; making it one of the best uses.

blackberry and apple crumble

Clean, core and slice apples. Add washed blackberries and apple or pear concentrate (or some sugar syrup to sweeten). Partly cook the mixture until the apples and blackberries start to break down, then pour into a pie dish. Cover with a mix of flour, butter and sugar, roughly equal weights, with a little vanilla extract and a minute amount of milk to make a crumb texture, top with nutmeg and/or cinnamon. Then put in the top of a hot oven, 200°C/400°F/gas mark 6, to just lightly brown. Serve with custard.

Gooseberries *(Ribes uva-crispa var. reclinatum)*

Often known as only hard green bullets these are much underrated; their range of flavour, colour and size is wide, and they are not as bird-palatable as most soft fruit. They will grow on most soils, dislike waterlogging and hate stagnant conditions, though they don't mind a bit of shade. Much more controllable than raspberries or the blackberry clan, and more compact, they can be trained to be cordons or espaliers, shaped as goblets and grown on high or low stems. But the whole point is to remove congestion to allow picking! And equally to allow the sun and air to enter.

Gooseberries wanted just for juice or jam can be grown as a stool, like raspberries or blackcurrants, but then become unpickable. For choice fruits for dessert, you need to hard prune to spurs on a main framework. This pruning is often left till last, even until the buds move, as bullfinches rob their buds if they are left unprotected. Summer pruning keeps them open and, if they are well trained, can be done with shears.

Gooseberries do suffer from a mildew, which if bad ruins the crop but often just disfigures the fruits; the whitish capping can be removed if you rub them with a soapy sponge. The best varieties are not mildew-resistant – some hate sulphur, which prevents mildew – and most of the good ones are thorny. However, a large number can be grown in a small space if hard pruned as cordons, and as long as they get a breeze and damp roots to keep the mildew down. They are very hungry for wood ashes and seaweed sprays; mulches are useful; and they grow well through a background cover of *Limnanthes douglasii* – which usefully self-seeds, grows through winter protecting the soil and dies away as the gooseberries are ripening. They can be grown in big containers and even moved under cover for cropping, or for holding a crop on longer in a cool, dry, safe place.

Varieties

I love 'Langley Gage', an old small white; there are countless reds, greens, whites and even clear yellows.

Harvest

Gooseberries benefit from early thinning – the tiniest fruits can be used to make tarts and jams – and a second thinning – more treats – before the main crop is picked for jam, for which the fruits are often better taken unripe. Leave the choicest for use in desserts, fresh – they can get huge.

RIGHT **Gooseberries can be brought under cover for an earlier crop.**

Preserving and use

Gooseberries are too seedy to be dried, though their sieved pulp and juice can go in leather. Some of the best can be frozen, using a neat trick: once they're frozen, run them in a potato rumbler peeler for a few seconds and remove all the tops, tails and hairs, leaving them smooth like grapes – or slip off their skins as they defrost.

The cold extracted juice makes a fantastic sorbet, and the choicest berries go well in compotes or cooked in sponges. Of course the best-known dish to Anglo-cuisine enthusiasts is gooseberry fool, but to the French their name, *groseille à maquereau* – 'currant for mackerel' – is for their acid sauce to go with greasy mackerel. A tip on eating them fresh: if you nip out the flower end with your fingers and squeeze the fruit while sucking at the hole, you can squirt the contents into your mouth, leaving the tough skin to throw away.

Gooseberries can be bottled. Their juice can be a bit acid if too young, and not acid enough if fully ripe – and not that strong a flavour for a good syrup or squash. Gooseberry jam is excellent, as the skins can be enjoyed, but the seeds of some varieties annoy, so the jelly is better. One important point: the best jam is without doubt green, unripe-gooseberry jam; if you want it to stay green,

use no berries from red ripening varieties and keep the heat down to just enough to cook them. It's wonderful. Gooseberry juice from green berries can also be used in place of lemon juice. Gooseberries can be used in mixed preserves, pickled, chutneyed and made into all sorts of sauces, cheeses, butters and leathers, but they are always a bit seedy – and too much so for crystallising.

Redcurrants and whitecurrants *(Ribes sativum)*

These are, in many ways, very similar to gooseberries, but they are not thorny and do not suffer mildew; however, they are robbed mercilessly by birds so need good nets or a cage. Generally regarded as garnishes, they are not often enjoyed as the fruit they are; fully ripe they are less acid and have a good clean taste, though they're still small and seedy. Their main culinary use is for their juice – acid and clear red, or whitish – which is an excellent substitute for lemon juice for sharpening up jams, jellies and sauces, sweet and savoury. These fruits should be more widely grown.

They like any soil and site, even cropping on north walls, they can be pruned to any shape or form and they crop relentlessly whatever you do. When, after twenty years, the top has died, a new one can be grown from the roots, which seem to go on forever.

gooseberry and strawberry liqueur

Take enough under-ripe, acidic green gooseberries to fill half a bottle and prick each one. Half-fill a wide necked bottle with the gooseberries and half with ripe but firm strawberries. Pour in overproof white rum or brandy. Seal and store in a cool place and invert the bottle daily for two months. After about two months, sediment will collect in the bottom of the bottle. It is then ready to decant into a clean bottle to which sugar syrup is added to taste.

A delicious love potion – if each of you drink half a bottle, together

They can be grown and cropped in big pots and even brought on early or protected under cover, and if kept on the plant and under cover – away from birds – the crop can be held till into the New Year. I have had them outside in October. Hard winter and summer pruning back to spurs on a framework and a goblet shape is probably the best option, but, as said, they will take any shape you imagine and still crop. But a cage is necessary; netting will have too many trapped birds. They do not need heavy feeding; some wood ashes and mulches are good, as are seaweed sprays.

Varieties

The many reds vary a little, and the whites are reds with no – or just a touch of – pink colour.

Harvest

Don't pick them if they can be left, as they hang so well; then for juicing they can be taken, sprigs and all, but for freezing it is best to pick off the best berries individually and then roughly pick the rest.

Preserving and use

These currants do not make a very good jam, jelly, juice or sorbet on their own, but act brilliantly as a carrier for others – so cherries in redcurrant jelly is fabulous, as is raspberry and redcurrant jelly, and also chokeberry (*Aronia*) and redcurrant jelly.

Currants can be bottled, but are so easy to freeze there seems little point. And if you juice and then freeze them in small packs such as plastic cups, they'll be available whenever needed, which is often before this year's crop is ready. Currants are too seedy to dry, or to crystallise, but their acid juice is so useful it can end up in everything else that needs more bite, from pickles to leather. Sadly, although they go well with other flavours, on their own currants make poor wine and liqueurs, or love potions – though mint-sauce whitecurrant jelly is close to one if you love roast lamb.

Blackcurrants (*Ribes nigrum*)

Very different from redcurrants and whitecurrants, these are rarely eaten as fresh fruits, are drier and have a very strong flavour that overwhelms anything else. But given sugar they are wonderful, and they're full of vitamins and very productive – and bird-palatable. A cage is necessary, and the plants need to be at least two or three paces apart. They crop rather well even in heavy shade – though

RIGHT **Nothing is easier to train and crop than redcurrants.**

summer pudding

Take 2 pounds (900g) of mixed berries, such as raspberries, blueberries, halved strawberries and redcurrants. Place into a pan with 2 tablespoons apple concentrate or sugar syrup and simmer for just 2 minutes. You want the fruit to soften but still remain whole. Drain off most of the juice and reserve.

Line a 1-pint pudding basin with clingfilm. Take 6–8 slices of thinly sliced white bread. Dip these in the juices as you go and use to line the basin, cutting slices in half where need be to fit the mould. Tip the fruit in, packing it in tightly and top with another slice of dipped bread. Add the syrup left from the fruits, pressing the lot down firmly to exclude any air bubbles but not to the point where it all becomes runny, then place a clean greased block of wood on top and a weight on top of that and place in the fridge overnight. It will set overnight and can be turned out onto a plate and served with cream or cold custard.

obviously at the expense of sweetness. For jam-making fruits, a mixture of full sun and shade is better than either alone. The plants are very hungry and love rich, heavy soils that are well fed and watered, with seaweed sprays and thick mulches, especially of well-rotted manure or feathers. And they need ruthless pruning: everything more than a couple of years old should be cut out and new shoots grown from the stool set deep in the ground; they'll grow up as shoots. If the plants are happy and hard pruned, huge fruits the size of cherries can be produced and in very heavy yields. An interesting way to pick and prune is to do both together: cut out, at or near ground level, the entire branch that is cropping, take it away and pick in comfort – or stand it in water in a cool place to keep for longer. Blackcurrants can be grown and cropped in containers and brought indoors for earlier crops, or stored in the cool for later ones held on the bush a tad longer.

Varieties

There is very little to choose between most varieties. The Jostaberry is a near relation (a blackcurrant-gooseberry hybrid) with the same flavour on a bigger more permanent frame – more like a thornless, blackcurrant-tasting, giant gooseberry bush.

Preserving and use

Blackcurrants freeze well and are good for compotes and sorbets. They need to be bottled in apple or another juice as they are so dry on their own, and their juice really has to be extracted with hot water and sugar. Extra liquid – apple/redcurrant/whitecurrant/ lemon juice or verjuice – is needed for the jam, as again the fruits alone are too dry; they go rather well with strawberries and surprisingly well with lemon. The jam always sets, as does the jelly – and indeed I often find I have inadvertently let the syrup and the squash set on me when they're chilled or frozen. The pulp remaining after you've made jelly is still good enough to go in a leather or cheese, and the fruits could be crystallised, though they often go hard. They are also too hard to dry well, but the leather made with apple is one of the best. The commercial juice is hard to replicate, but you can boil unripe or ripe blackcurrants with redcurrant juice and a lot of water and sugar to get a similar squash; do not make it too strong: the commercial stuff is often less than 10% or even 5% fruit juice! Blackcurrants have too strong a flavour to be used in pickles and chutneys, but do make a fair and well-coloured wine and an excellent liqueur, which is the base for a warming winter toddy. Their vinegar is one of the most health-giving.

blackcurrant liqueur

Wash a couple of handfuls of blackcurrants, prick each with a needle and tip into a bottle. Add high proof white rum until full, seal and refrigerate. Remove from the fridge every-day and invert the bottle a couple of times to gently mix. After a month or so strain off the alcohol, pass through a muslin-lined sieve or clean coffee filter and pour into a clean bottle up to the halfway mark. Top up with an equal amount of sugar syrup and a little apple concentrate, if you like. It is best left for a month or two for the flavour to mellow and develop. See pages 70–71.

Blueberries *(Vaccinium corymbosum)*

An absolute must and unbelievably easy, blueberries are productive, healthy, tasty and, apart from the birds, problem-free as long as they are kept moist with rainwater (not tap water). Happy in large containers of acid compost, these like ericaceous mixes full of peat and always kept moist. They need very little feeding but loads of water and, if grown in containers, they need little pruning, except perhaps to prevent them from overcropping or to get fewer, bigger fruits. These are very bird-palatable so must be netted, and in the case of several varieties can be cropped over a long season.

Blueberries can be moved under cool cover for earlier or later crops, but resent a hot dry position indoors or out. They can even go to the front garden for late autumn when their foliage becomes a magnificent show. Although they are self-fertile in theory, bigger better crops come when several varieties are grown near one another; there are high and low forms, rabbit-eye and hybrids; and in their moist acid conditions they can be underplanted with the almost prostrate cranberries for a second crop. An old bath makes a good-size container for three plants of each – and can be set almost flush in the ground if thought an eyesore.

Preserving and use

Commercially, blueberries are dried, but I've never produced enough to do this as they are eaten too quickly; most spare ones go in the freezer but even then don't stay long. They can be jammed, though this seems a waste as they are good fresh dessert fruits, and good frozen fruits for compotes – and, of course, for cooking in muffins. Again I imagine blueberries could be used in all sorts of ways – I believe the native Americans smoked them to preserve them – but their elusive flavour would be lost by most methods, and there would be little reason to put them in chutneys or pickles. I've not made the wine or the liqueur, but it sounds feasible; perhaps any readers with huge crops can suggest the better use.

Grapes *(Vitis spp.)*

As yet, most gardeners have not understood how to cope with grapevines, so they are grown far less than they should be: grapes are easy to produce, store better than you expect and are easy to process – and to make wine from, of course. If you want to grow them outside in the ground, there are only a few good choices and then you will have huge crops – sometimes. If you grow them outdoors in tubs, you get smaller more manageable crops but of the same few varieties. Under cover it is not good to have a permanent vine, but many can be brought in and out in tubs. This gives many

FROM LEFT TO RIGHT **Grapes look odd as you start to dry them. Home-grown raisins now finished off in a warm oven. Too dry is no good, stop while they are still firm.**

varieties, a longer season and no build-up of pests and diseases. And with some moved indoors and some out, and some stored in bottles, you can spread the fresh grape harvest over more than half the year.

Vines need poor soil, warm sunny sites and psychopathic pruning. The crueller you treat them, the better. Cut almost everything off in autumn as soon as the leaves start to fall. Build up spurs on a frame by cutting every shoot back to two buds, except for shoots left to make the frame bigger or renew it. In spring, as the shoots break, watch as they lengthen; after three and never more than five leaves, if they are going to flower it will have appeared. Pull off all shoots that have no flowers. Of those left, choose the best-placed stems, especially those breaking from lowermost, to be this year's crop-carrying ones, and pull off all others or reduce them to one or two leaves long. Reduce the flowers to one bunch – no more – on each. The canes should be no closer than a foot or so apart, and tied in place. Once the stems have grown another three to five leaves, cut off the ends, and then

later shear off any replacement shoots that spurt out, thus concentrating all the vine's energy into the fruits.

In tubs, reduce the vine to a squat frame with only a couple of spurs, each with a couple or three stumps of this year's canes each only two buds long. When these shoot, select the four or six best with flowers to be the fruiting canes, train these up a tall bamboo and cut off anything beyond or spurting out sideways.

You can cut grapevines to near the ground like roses, or leave them to ramble over trees – although on these the fruits will become unpickable if not stolen by birds. They can also be shaped to any form you might imagine, on a wall or wires. For dessert use, a wall is almost essential, and one vine will cover any size you want, and crop heavily; I've had eight gallons of juice from one! But for a sensible vineyard, vines are about right at two to three strides apart on wires, with a path at least a good stride or two wide, and the framework should consist of one branch running along a low wire with spurs built on it. This should sit a foot or less from the ground, so the fruits will be between waist and knee height, with the canes tied, and cut off, at another wire at waist height. Every so often, a young strong cane from near the first spur is retained in winter to replace the old worked-out branch and spurs.

Outdoors, do nothing other than keep off the birds. If you have vines in tubs, bring them in sequentially from late winter, inspect carefully for scale and so on, and keep some of the same variety back in cold places for later crops. Water well once they shoot, feed weekly and ventilate well. Watch for wasps! Do not even consider anything as time-wasting as cutting out individual berries. If mildew threatens, puff them over with sulphur dust; this is allowed and works well.

Varieties

Outdoors 'Siegerrebe', a rosy red, is so early that the wasps bother it; with a warm wall it will give you grapes in August. It does not like chalky soil, which is unusual. 'Boskoop Glory', black, good for both dessert fruit and wine, has proved immensely reliable, cropping well for twenty-five years; it ripens in September and into October. No others have proved worth growing for dessert fruit, though 'Léon Millot', 'Maréchal Joffre', 'Triomphe d'Alsace' and 'Seibel 13053', all reds, have proved good croppers for juice or wine. (The first two also dry to fair, if seedy, currants – though the relatively seedless 'Zante', the true currant, can be got if you want the real thing.) If you have poor taste buds, the strawberry grape is a

massive cropper; it will cover a big tree with fruit! Under cover, preferably in tubs, 'Siegerrebe' is worth having as it can crop in June and is so tasty. 'Madresfield Court', black, and 'Muscat Hamburg', black, are the most luscious and well flavoured. 'Black Hamburg' and 'Regent', black, are excellent. The seedless 'Flame', red, is odd eating but good, and makes a chewy, pinky-red raisin; 'Perlette', a seedless white, is also good for drying as a sultana. The seedless 'Himrod', amber, makes a good dessert, a lovely juice and an excellent sultana. The most reliable white is 'Golden Chasselas' ('Chasselas d'Or'/'Royal Muscadine') and this will make a good wine; 'Buckland's Sweetwater' is another good dessert white, if small, as is 'Foster's Seedling'. Most of the white vines on offer are poor eaters and far too disease-prone for wine. There is an enormous number of grapes, and I've only grown four dozen, so forgive me if your favourite is not here.

Harvest

With the earliest, watch for translucency in the berry. With the majority, leave them until the weather, or the birds – or, under cover, the wasps – threaten to take the lot. Grapes do not rot quickly if cut dry and kept in a fruit room suspended by their stalk or in nets. The seedless ones with solid texture, such as Himrod and 'Flame', can be picked and chilled in bags in your fridge and can keep till the New Year. Surprisingly, most grapes can hang on the vines well into winter if they do not get robbed or go mouldy; those with loose open bunches resist rots better. But leaving bunches on the vine suppresses the next growths, encourages pests and disease, and may be difficult to fit in with pruning! However, grape bunches can be cut with a length of stem and kept fresh in bottles of water stood in a cool dark safe place. Some will keep for months – I have had some make it till Easter! Once a week, remove, cut a bit off the end of the stem and replace the water; also remove any suspicious berries.

Preserving and use

Grapes don't freeze well, becoming baggy, tough skins of seeds full of water, even if packed in syrup, and they make only fair sorbets. They can be bottled, though it is barely worth it. It is, however, well worth squeezing them for their juice, which does freeze well and is fantastic to have year round. A mix of juice from the sweetest indoor desserts that are going over and the more acid outdoor ones is best. Pick out mouldy grapes or those with brown withered shanks, as these give off tastes. Even the unripe juice is worth having, as it can be used instead of lemon or whitecurrant juice.

Grapes rather surprisingly dry really well and easily; of course seedless ones seem preferable but they are few, and not all are well flavoured or productive. You can squeeze or cut the fruits and pick out the seeds (this is tedious), or pick the smallest berries, as these are often less seedy than the huge. I dry them as they come, only washed, and the seeds are taken as part of them – crunchy, hey. Black grapes make good raisins, muscat grapes the best, white ones make sultanas, and rosé grapes dry reddish and best of all. This method should not be underrated: drying grapes is quick and easy and the best use after juicing – other than wine, that is.

Grapes are not jammed as they're too seedy, but they do make a good jelly that usually sets. A thin syrup can be made for use as a squash from the stronger-flavoured reds but is less good from whites. Acid grape juice can be useful for adding tartness to preserves, cheeses and butters but grapes are not usually a main constituent as they have so little body. The same goes for candying and crystallising, although it might be worth trying crunchy seedless varieties such as 'Flame'. For wine-making, see pages 68–69 – and, of course, you'd expect grapes to make nice liqueurs and love potions, but sadly they don't; however, 'Siegerrebe' does make an excellent sweet dessert wine.

SUNDRY FRUITS

Kiwi fruit *(Actinidia deliciosa)*

These can be infuriating, refusing to crop for years and then throwing barrow-loads. Ideally grown and hard pruned as espaliers, they may crop regularly if both male and female are grown, but this requires space and a lot of training. Or, just left to ramble, they cover trees and sometimes crop hugely. Some will hang on till the New Year, becoming soft if frosted but remaining edible. In the fruit room they keep in paper-lined trays for another month or more, and in the fridge for up six months or so, making them valuable sources of fresh fruit in spring.

Kiwi jam does not set properly and the jelly is worse; both can be made with apple added but then are still annoyingly full of little black seeds. Kiwis could be bottled or dried, but the centre is tough already; I've not tried. I guess a leather could be made, or a cheese, but the taste is distinct and unlikely to mix well. The juice, made by sugaring overnight and straining, is okay but not to everyone's taste; nor is the syrup. However, the sorbet is excellent and is a very good use for them – try it with chilli! You can try kiwi wine…

kiwi sorbet

Take kiwis once they have become too soft to enjoy and carefully peel them, cover with the same weight of sugar syrup and gently warm until completely softened (the core may remain firm). Pass through a fine sieve; cool and churn in an ice-cream maker if you have one, otherwise partly freeze in a metal dish. Every hour or so, remove and whisk to aerate the mix and prevent ice crystals forming, thus freezing to a smooth, fluffy sorbet. Depending on how full/powerful your freezer, this should take between 4 and 6 hours.

A glut of kiwis is best stored and used till they soften, then made into sorbet

economical marmalade

First of all, any citrus can be made into marmalade but some have more bitter skins, or rather pith, than others, so traditionally oranges and lemons are preferred. However, I like that bitterness so I save all citrus skins from organic sources in the freezer. These are then very finely sliced and simmered in apple concentrate and mixed fifty-fifty with orange juice so that it covers them amply. Once the flesh is very soft, then the pan and ingredients are weighed, with the weight of the pan subtracted and the same weight of sugar added (so the weight of the citrus ingredient), brought to a simmer till it clears and then jarred and sealed.

Figs (*Ficus carica*)

The figs we grow do not set seeds, nor do they need pollinating. The plants are hardy and, when grown in the ground, will sometimes produce huge gluts. These can be exchanged for more regular crops if you remove every fig, big or tiny, after the leaves fall. The best figs are borne on short jointed wood; long jointed shoots should be pruned out unless needed for the frame. Thinning the crop is essential if fewer, bigger fruits are wanted.

Traditionally, figs were planted in brick boxes; I use ex-washing-machine drums – but just planting against a warm wall usually helps constrict their roots. Never feed or use muck and so on near figs in the ground, and be wary of letting them have water: you want them growing in dry poor soil or you get all leaf and no fruit. They are far better and more controllable in tubs, and as dozens of varieties are available, growing them this way along with using some cover could give you a long season. Indeed, if you use a bit of cunning and have several, both earlies and lates, and move them under cover, you can get three crops a year and have almost non-stop fresh figs.

But, more realistically, by just bringing them in during early spring you can expect good crops in summer and autumn. The latest figs may hold on – but if it's warm they'll drop, and if it's cold they'll rot. Put a drop of olive oil on the eye to speed ripening, and then enclose the fruit in a muslin bag so, if it drops, you get it before the birds. Eat as soon as the skin splits; ripe ones can be stored in a fridge for a few days but rapidly go off.

Figs can be bottled in syrup, when they benefit from some whitecurrant or lemon juice or verjuice, or they can be made into a syrupy jam (though it's hard to set). You cannot dry UK varieties very easily; if you do, they shrivel to an even smaller size than the commercial seedy ones. For the same reason, I guess candying is out, though maybe not. I have never made the wine – the effects could be dreadful! – nor a liqueur; I guess fresh figs would store well in brandy and syrup.

Mulberries (*Morus nigra*)

Source of a wonder food not yet vaunted, these are big trees, though they can be pruned or pollarded cruelly and survive; the white are hacked for silkworms. If you have space, one of these trees is traditional in the middle of a lawn, with a seat around the trunk. Their biggest problem is dry soil, which causes poor crops of miserable fruits. Mulberries drop over a period and are not so good if picked, so put down sheets, if not lawn, underneath. Fresh, the black is the common one and is much better than the white, though the red from North America is very good.

Mulberries can be dried, but need careful treatment or they mould first. If frozen they need to be packed in syrup. They can be bottled as if they were blackberries; for this they are better a tad under-ripe so will need to be picked – overripe ones will break down. So as not to lose their flavour, use sugar syrup. Not particularly good for jam, mulberries need apple purée to set and are not a brilliant flavour for this. If you had enough they could be made into a cheese or leather, but again the taste would be lacking. I have preserved them in rum and syrup and they were more interesting than delicious; the liqueur was not that wonderful either. Just eat them fresh with clotted cream and shortbread, okay?

Citrus

Surprisingly, there are a lot of these grown in the UK, especially lemons, and although tender and pest-prone, citrus are tough and determined to crop. And unless thinned they tend to overcrop, so be warned or you'll end up with a huge number of mini fruits. These are, for once, not so problematical as they can be turned into excellent marmalade; however, overcropping still weakens the bushes.

Citrus must be tub-grown so they can overwinter under cover somewhere cool, frost-free, bright and airy and not too dry. Not your living room, is it? A thermostatically-kept-just-frost-free greenhouse is perfect, and even an unheated one, given extra glazing, will get you through most winters. However, to get good fruit, which mostly ripen in winter, you need some warmth. Being too dry does not suit them, so mist them. They like well-drained, neutral compost, and to be very well fed – indeed spoilt – with liquid feed and copious watering in the sunny half of the year, and kept just moist when it's dull. And they always like rainwater.

In winter, be careful not to let their feet get cold and wet, or they rot; err on the side of caution and keep the soil just moist – feel maturing fruits and if they start to feel limp, not firm, then the soil is too dry, or the roots have already gone. Too cold and damp and they mould, or drop leaves and fruits, or look sad and yellow. Too warm and dry and they suffer loads of pests. Too hot all the time and the fruits will not colour but stay green.

citrus liqueur

This is an excellent use for small citrus fruits that are removed when thinning. Wash, pierce with a needle and put into a bottle with some other soft fruit, such as redcurrants, raspberries or strawberries as the combination is better than the citrus alone. Fill the bottle with white rum and stand in the cool and agitate daily. After three months, decant the rum and mix with sugar syrup to taste, bottle and leave to mature. The fruits strained out can go on to make a fruit leather – though, again, you must be careful they do not make it too bitter for your taste.

Once the frosts are passed, they are hardened off and live outside till the frosts return; they will need a lot of feeding and watering and seaweed sprays. However, don't worry: they will crop. Most citrus will ripen in winter, earlier or later depending on their history as much as on their variety. Leaving ripe fruits on the bush suppresses the next crop; stripping all off early brings on the next. So if you have two bushes of the same variety, treat them differently and they will crop over a longer time between them. Water stress, followed by reviving, can cause extra flowering; of course the stress will also have caused any prior sets to drop!

Varieties

Lemons are easy, productive and useful, and with several different varieties. 'Meyer's', 'Lisbon' and 'Eureka' are good, and you are rarely without fruit and have the odd glut. Kumquats and tangerines are also easy and give lots of fruits. Obviously small trees in tubs cannot carry many full-size grapefruits or big oranges, so these are less worth having – unless you can afford big trees and have the space for them. *Poncirus trifoliata,* Japanese bitter orange, is a hardy thorny shrub that does, eventually, have little orange-like fruits, but these are not at all nice even as marmalade, although edible and presumably liked in Japan. However, hybrids of this with other citrus may prove better. Do not grow citrus from seeds; they will crop, but it can take decades – I know: it took twenty-three years for my 'Ortanique' to fruit.

Harvest

Take the very smallest fruitlets for pot-pourris; small fruitlets add zest to liqueurs; and small fruits with any juiciness become eligible for marmalade. It is worth cutting fruits off, as pulling often damages the skin round the neck. Citrus can be kept in a fridge for weeks, or even months – slowly shrivelling. Without chilling they go mouldy quickly, especially where they can't breathe, so either lay them on shredded paper or suspend them in nets.

Preserving and use

Citrus were once preserved by being coated with sodium bicarbonate powder, but this was unsightly and spoiled the skins; I've not tried it. Citrus can be juiced very easily and the juice frozen; they can be made into excellent sorbets and ice-lollies. The best can be reduced to portions and frozen packed in syrup, or preserved in syrup, or liqueured – this last is very, very good. And, of course, citrus, or just their skins, make among the best candied and crystallised fruits – especially tiny tangerines and kumquats.

Candying chopped peel in bulk is a lot quicker than candying individual pieces, at all stages, and useful for exotic desserts and cake recipes.

Depending on your taste, you may already prefer 'bitter' or 'sweet' marmalades and citrus dishes. The flavour of the flesh and juice is different and often preferred if some of the zest and the rind is included (scratch it off with a fine grater); too much can add bitterness, as does much of the white pith. So prepare your fruits differently according to whether you want more or less 'bitterness'. Kumquats have small, thin-walled fruits with little pith; they can be eaten whole and are sometimes coated in chocolate as a treat – though this does not help them keep much longer.

When making marmalade, take into consideration that, unlike with most fruit, it is the citrus' skins, pith and seeds that have most to give, and these take longer to cook, so simmer marmalade for longer than you would most fruits for jam or jelly. The peel must be prepared however you want it in the marmalade, so usually slice it very thin, or thicker, or cut it into chunks, or mince it, or whatever you like for the texture you are after. The skin of sweet oranges will not make a clear marmalade jelly. The pith of grapefruit and of bitter or Seville oranges cooks translucent, while other citrus-peel pith tends to stay white. Do not take the seeds out until they have had their goodness extracted, or take them out at the start but put them back in a wee cloth bag for extraction.

Mini citrus lollies

Pour a fifty-fifty mix of orange juice and sugar syrup into an ice-cube tray. Take a handful of wooden kebab skewers, cut off the sharp end, push the end into a raisin (to weigh it down, also a nice bonus to chew on at the end!) and place one in each cube. Freeze the mini lollies, turn out into a plastic bag or container and have ready in the freezer for those hot summer days.

LEFT **Lemons are easy in tubs under cover and crop almost all year round**

lemon meringue

Make a sweet shortcrust pastry. Rub 4 ounces (110g) cubed, cold butter into 7 ounces (200g) plain flour. Stir in 3 ounces (75g) caster sugar, a pinch of salt and bind together with an egg yolk and 1–2 tablespoons cold water. Rest in the fridge for half an hour, then roll out and use to line a fluted flan ring. Rest again in the fridge then bake blind: line with greaseproof paper, fill with baking beans and bake for 12–15 minutes, 180°C/350°F/gas mark 4. Remove the paper and beans and cook for another 5 minutes until a pale biscuit colour. Cool and chill.

Melt about 4 ounces (110g) dark chocolate in a bain-marie and pour into the pastry case, swirling it to evenly coat the base. Chill. (This coating will set, keeping the base dry and crisp.)

Then start to make your lemon curd by finely grating the zest and juice of 2 large lemons. Place into a heavy pan or double boiler with 3 ounces(75g) butter, 8 ounces (225g) sugar and 6 egg yolks. Heat gently, stirring all the time until thickened. Cool slightly then pour into the pastry case.

For the meringue topping, whisk 2 egg whites until fluffy then gradually whisk in 2 ounces (50g) caster sugar, whisking very well between each addition to make a stiff, glossy meringue. Spoon on top of the cooled lemon curd and bake in a medium oven, 150°C/300°F/gas 3, for 15 minutes until golden and set. Serve cold.

Rose hips, rowans and elderberries

All of these are often freely available in abundance, and are well worth harvesting for turning into jam or jelly for the vitamins, anthocyanins and minerals they carry. Rose hips – from any rose, but the fleshier are better – can be halved and the hairy seeds removed, then the fleshy bits simmered, with just enough water to cover them until they're broken down. Then sieve, mix with the same weight of apple purée and their combined weight of sugar, reboil and pot. Or you can cut them in half, boil with double the amount of water, strain through a fine bag to remove the hairy bits and combine with the same weight of sugar to make a syrup – best kept refrigerated or bottled.

Both rowans and elderberries are good boiled and strained for a jelly, easily made with apple concentrate. Elderberry jelly is thought to be especially health-giving. Rowans can be puréed and are good included in cheeses, especially to go with savoury dishes. Elderberry combines well with other bland cheeses such as apple, and does make a very good wine. I've not tried making rose-hip liqueur but it sounds worth a go. Some rose-hip syrup I had became the wine, not unlike a plum wine – hazy and highly flavoured – and then it became the vinegar, which I still have as a curio.

Everything else

It is amazing what other fruits you can find that can be eaten or preserved for later use. Fuchsia berries – as is known, all common varieties – are actually edible and their jelly has long been made in competitions at fuchsia societies. The ripe purple berries, which have tiny seeds and are not unlike bland stoneless Morello cherries, make a good jelly, especially with apple concentrate.

Be very careful, cross-reference and make sure, but in fact very many species of *Aronias, Berberis, Celtis, Cornus, Crataegus, Elaegnus, Gaultheria, Gaylussacia, Hippophae, Mahonia, Myrtus, Shepherdia, Sorbus, Vaccinium* and *Viburnum* have fruits that are edible when cooked. They can be made into jellies, syrups and cheeses and – possibly the greatest health potential of all, as they're so easily consumable – liqueurs and fruit vinegars. These are all particularly high in vitamins and anthocyanins. Some of these fruits need apple concentrate to set if you want a jam. And remember, as I say, some are edible, others are not.

Nuts

Not many of us have room for nuts, as they generally make huge trees – even hazels. However, they can be scrumped where they are in abundance and are very low-maintenance crops if you do have the space to plant them. They have very high protein and fat levels, as well as containing lots of minerals, and in green terms are probably the best crops to grow. To blanch them for dessert or cooking, drop them – shelled – into boiling water for a minute or so, and then into cold, when the skins can be slipped off.

Hazel (*Corylus spp.*)

This includes the similar bigger cobnut and the better-sheathed filbert. These are good crops for poor dry sites, preferably a long way from squirrels and wood pigeons. The named varieties are much bigger nuts than the wild, save the tiny delicious red-skinned filbert. They, in theory, can be trained and hard pruned back to horizontal cartwheel forms, but I've not heard of it in living memory; just cut out the twiggy stuff at the base and strong verticals that threaten to choke the centre. Before the crop falls, cut underneath with a mower, collecting all the leaves and dead nuts. Then, before the squirrels get them, shake the trees and pick up all the nuts; later, sort them and keep them in sieves or nets in a dry, airy place to cure. They will keep in excellent condition till spring. If you want to keep them for longer, they are best stored in their shells packed in jars of dry salt. They do slowly go off, but I've had some still edible years later.

The second crop is the one you steal back from the squirrels. They put many of the nuts finger depth down near the trees, so by vigorously raking the ground once all are apparently gone you can unearth hundreds more. These, being damp, are best eaten right away or shelled and processed as soon as possible.

The shelled nuts keep sealed in a jar in the fridge for some weeks, but are safer roasted with salt or honey – or even smoked – and then sealed and packed in the freezer till required, when they can be oven refreshed. Or they can be blanched, ground to a coarse flour in a processor and made into macaroons, which keep well in a biscuit tin or frozen. Or you can blanch them, chop them and mix them with home-made raisins in your own chocolate bar. (So here is the place to use seedy raisins.)

Roasted nuts

Take a quantity of shelled mixed nuts, including hazel and cob. (To shell your own nuts, blanch in boiling water for a few minutes, cool slightly then slip their skins off). Pound together some salted anchovies, garlic, smoked paprika and peppercorns to a smooth paste. Tip into a bowl with the nuts and mix together, ensuring you coat all the nuts. Spread them out in a single layer onto a large greased baking tray and roast in a hot oven 200°C/400°F/gas mark 6, for ten minutes or so until golden. Cool and store in an airtight jar or container in the fridge to keep fresh if not eating in a hurry.

Chestnuts (*Castanea sativa*)

These make very big trees, are slow to crop and only crop well after two good summers, so the nuts may be better scrumped when seen going to waste. If well dried, they may keep till late winter, but are not very good long-term keepers in a temperate climate such as in the UK, where they tend to be small and moist. They can, once dry, be packed in salt and sawdust to keep longer. They are traditionally roasted; prick them first if you don't want explosions. Or they can be shelled, ground to a fine flour, boiled with sugar and vanilla and bottled as crème de marron glacé, which is a bit like chocolate spread. Interestingly enough, lime fruits – as in linden (*tilia*) trees – were once roasted and ground with some of their flowers and sugar to make a chocolate (but it did not keep well).

Walnuts (*Juglans regia*)

These are huge trees eventually, and slow to crop, but very useful if you have the space. Walnuts are not so easy to scrump, as usually all are spoken for. Get them as soon as they fall – wear rubber gloves – and remove the decaying husk before it stains the nuts. Then dry them in single layers as rapidly as possible without heating them up. Some people wash them, quickly, so the shells don't open, to make them prettier, and scrub off any husk which may start to rot. I rub them with wood ashes, then pack them in a mixture of wood ashes, dry salt and sawdust, and they keep well till the next summer. Or you can shell, blanch and chop them, mix them with coffee syrup and then freeze for later inclusion in cakes. Traditionally, of course, walnuts were pickled. To do this, pick nuts when a pin can still be pushed through them without resistance, then soak them, in their fledgling shells and green husks, for a day or three in a brine of a pound of salt per gallon of water (500g per 5 litres). Then drain, replace with fresh brine and leave for a week. Then drain again, and lay the nuts on oiled trays in the air and light for a day to turn black. Pack them into jars, cover with hot, sweet, spiced vinegar and seal; store for at least a month or three before eating. They also make an excellent aperitif liqueur.

hazel chocolate bar

You can use raisins
and dried cherries in
your chocolate too...

Take hazel or cobnuts and shell them, then drop into boiling water in small batches for a few minutes, rescue and slip the skins off, cool and dry. Melt the chocolate (you can use a bar each time of your favourite milk or dark chocolate) very slowly and carefully in a bain marie or double saucepan. Pour a thin layer of chocolate into a chilled metal dish pre-lined with buttered aluminium foil and swirl it around to cover the bottom and partway up the sides and place in the freezer to chill.

Melt more chocolate and stir in gently about one quarter to a third of its own weight of the blanched dried nuts then pour the mixture into the chilled chocolate 'tray' you have made and return to the freezer to set. Once set, melt more chocolate and apply a sealing coat on top of the chilled mixture and return to the freezer. Once solid through, remove the slab of chocolate, peel off the foil and cut the slab with a sharp solid knife into squares by belting the back of the knife with a mallet. Alternatively, do the same with an ice-cube tray to get individual chunks.

Almonds (*Prunis dulcis var. amygdalis*)

Flowering almonds and sweet almonds grown near them – or near to, and so pollinated by, peaches or nectarines – have bitter kernels you should not eat. However, sweet almonds do grow and crop in the UK; they are effectively peach trees, and the crop can be huge. If on their own, they are sweet and need to be husked and the nuts in the shells well dried and packed in salt, when they keep for months. Or you can shell, blanch and keep them in the fridge – or, even better, grind them with butter, sugar and vanilla to make marzipan. You will not get it as smooth or white as the commercial stuff, but it will taste great. As with hazels, bits of these nuts go well with home-made raisins sealed in chocolate.

LEFT A handful at least saved from the squirrels.
OPPOSITE **Picking your own nuts actually means grubbing about in the leaves.**

walnut liqueur

Pick green walnuts so early that a big needle can be easily pushed through them and do so to each a couple of times. Place the pierced nuts in a jar or wide-necked bottle and cover with either dark rum or brandy. Place in the fridge and, every day or so, gently agitate and return. After 3 months pour off the alcohol into another bottle and add to it the same volume of strong sugar syrup. Leave to mature for several months before drinking. If you wish, a variation is to re-soak the once used nuts in red wine for another 3 months and then mix this extract with the strong alcohol extract and yet more syrup.

Mushrooms

Although not grown deliberately by many gardeners, these are one of those crops that come with few at all or too many in a rush – especially to those who have applied mushroom farm compost as a mulch. Mushrooms are not difficult, if uneconomic, when you use the commercial kits, which are available for a very wide range of mushrooms, from the common shop ones to more exotic types such as Japanese shiitake and many different oyster mushrooms.

In theory, you can inoculate almost everything from your compost heap to your woodpile, and even your library, with some mushroom spawn or another. Several edible native wild mushrooms can be sown in your lawn with commercial spawn. Not very economical, these are only occasionally – but then very – successful, rather like the kits. The common and the oysters have often done well for me, but despite numerous attempts, not the shiitake, nor the truffles. Follow the instructions, especially with regard to watering, and you will get few or a glut. Pick them young and before they age and sporulate.

Although they can be frozen or bottled, mushrooms dry, store and reconstitute really well. Even more than with everything else, be sure of what you are handling and never mix in any doubtful ones, as the whole batch will then have to be suspect! Peeling may not be necessary for some young mushrooms but ensures cleanliness. Small ones can be dried whole. Or slice thinly – not as thin as you would slice fruit or vegetables, but a tad thicker, as mushrooms shrink more. Too thin and they become powdery and less useful. Hang them to dry on strings, or lay them on wire trays in a cool to warm oven, and then keep them in paper bags in glass jars, as you would herbs and seeds. They are quick to rehydrate. I have smoke-dried some to shrivelled relics which, when used sparingly, added that little something to bland winter casseroles.

Mushrooms can be pickled, or cooked in herbs and oil and bottled as antipasto. Or the fresh can be cooked with meals or bases you are making to freeze, such as ratatouille, pasta sauces and pizzas. And they can also be turned into a ketchup.

FROM LEFT TO RIGHT Peeled, de-stalked mushrooms are threaded by a needle.
Many mushrooms are threaded together.
Once the thread is hung they can be spaced out.

mushroom ketchup

Clean and peel large, not button, mushrooms, cut into slices and soak in brine overnight. Strain and rinse well and put into a saucepan with vinegar, any sort to your taste. Add spices; I suggest a spoonful apiece of ground cinnamon, ground ginger, ground mustard and ground paprika but some prefer cloves, mace and nutmeg. Simmer until the mushrooms become well softened, then press through a sieve. Freeze the ketchup, which is quite thin, in ice-cube trays and then store in a sealed bag in the freezer or put into small bottles and heat these to boiling point with the lids on (but not sealed tight, of course) for 20 minutes, sealing the tops tight before they cool.

mushroom antipasto

Clean the mushrooms and soak in brine for an hour or so, then rinse and drain. Put them into a saucepan with vinegar (wine or cider), a bay leaf, several cloves of garlic and some peppercorns, and a chilli if to your taste, and simmer until they are softened. Drain well and pack into jars, keep hot and fill with very hot olive oil and seal immediately. The vinegar drawn off can go to make mushroom ketchup or be used to add flavour to other dishes.

A great source of flavour and low-fat protein, mushrooms are a much under-utilised food that can be grown without light and dried so easily

Herbs and salad crops

PERENNIAL HERBS

These are greatly important for cooking well, but huge amounts of most of them are never wanted. Do you really need a bay tree, which gets as big as a small shed, when a lifetime's supply of bay leaves can be kept in one biscuit tin? The same goes for most other herbs, of which one good specimen or crop would give you a couple of years' supply. Many herbs, grown in a favoured spot and given some protection in harsh weather, can be cropped all year round, though the young spring and summer growths are more succulent. Generally, these don't mind being grown in a pot if freely drained and in a sunny spot; they can soon die in a humid or dark room or even a dingy greenhouse.

Rosemary, thyme, sage and marjoram (*Rosmarinus officinalis, Thymus, Salvia, Origanum vulgare*)

These are the typical perennial Mediterranean herbs, all needing that sunny, dry spot to have good flavour. Do not ever feed them, as this will give coarse rank growth; in pots their feeding must be minimal, though seaweed sprays are good, whether they're in pots or in the ground. Unless the weather is really severe, these herbs live on the patio; move them to cloches or cold frames only in worst weather, or to force early growth in spring. They need cutting back regularly to keep them tidy, and new plants need to be started every five years or so. For the thyme, the grey bushy sorts have the best flavour. For the sage, I prefer the red to the grey; the other variegated and coloured sages have less value. Golden marjoram is green in winter but useful all year round; it does in place of oregano. If you want true oregano, grow it in a frost-free greenhouse, as it is a tender perennial.

Harvest these herbs for processing just before the flowers form, or when there has been a flush of new growth after they've been cut back. They are best dried as single sprigs clipped to a line, then bagged and jarred. They can all be chopped and frozen in oil or water as herby ice cubes. But far better they – or even better their flowers – are picked and used to make exquisite liqueurs and tinctures. They're good for you, too.

Chives (*Allium schoenoprasum*)

These are far more useful than most people imagine; I pick vast amounts to include in salads, for omelettes and to make sauces. As they can be grown in pots, split and multiplied a hundredfold, they are easy to have in succession: bring pots into a warm, bright place to get fresh shoots almost all year round. With the ones in the open, cut alternate plants hard as you use them to spread the harvest; then, once the flowers appear, cut these off to prevent self-seeding. They are easy to dry: cut them like grass and spread them as a thin layer on a wire tray; once dried, cut them into sections.

Tarragon (*Artemisia dracunculus*)

This, if the true French – not the awful Russian – variety, is deliciously piquant. The plants do not do well in pots, though will survive in a sandy, well-drained compost, and they need splitting and replanting every third year or you lose them. Tarragon loses most flavour if dried. The fresh leaves are good in salads and with fish, but most of all you soak the young leafy shoots in vinegar. Make this super-strong, and then thin some down with more vinegar when needed.

Mint (*Mentha spp.*)

Needed all year round, especially for lamb and with new potatoes, mint does not require sun and does well in shade – and loves moisture. It tends to take over, so is often best grown in large tubs. The famous Bowles apple mint is reckoned the best-flavoured, but I prefer my own old Norfolk mint. Anyway, these can be had fresh most of the year; just dig up a root or two, pot them up, bring inside and force shoots and new leaves in the warmth. These are nicer than scraggy old leaves from wind-beaten outdoor survivors. Mint is always nice fresh for tisanes, but also can be made into liqueurs – and, of course, the sauce for lamb and new potatoes.

Mint sauce

Pick a flush of the top two leaves and the stem tips, and possibly the next lower leaves, well before flowering begins, ideally in the morning, and finely shred them into malt vinegar in a jar, in layers, alternately with layers of caster sugar. Keep in the fridge.

Alternatively, pick some mint, shred it into a cooling mixture of apple or whitecurrant jelly and cider vinegar, and bottle.

ANNUAL HERBS AND SALAD CROPS

These are mostly grown in rich, moist soil, and often they can be had over longer seasons if you sow them in batches, both in the ground and in pots. For this reason, most are rarely dried or frozen much. They are so valuable nutritionally, more should be eaten.

Basil (*Ocinum basilicum*)

This is an absolute must for many tomato dishes, and there are

many varieties with different flavours. These plants are very tender, so need to be sown in pots in warmth under cover and grown there, or later planted out, under cloches or in very warm sunny spots. Pot-grown plants expire as winter comes, even if cut back or kept warm. As soon as you have any harvestable amounts, freeze them in a well-sealed container – just the fresh stems and leaves, and as little handled as possible. The various basils can also be chopped into oil or water cubes and frozen and bagged separately. Unfortunately, basil does not dry with much flavour left. It can be included in tomato and pasta dishes made to be frozen – but make sure they are well sealed.

Herby ice cubes

Wash fresh herbs, chop very fine, mix into either stock, oil, butter or water and then put them into greased ice-cube trays. Freeze, remove and store in sealed bags in the freezer. (Do label each sort well!)

LEFT **Thyme and chives can be used in quantity, so grow plenty.**

flowerdew's super salad

I discovered that by blending many herbs and salad leaves I could make delicious salads with barely any lettuce or radish at all. The more different herbs I blended, the more pleasing the overall taste – though, of course, the very bitter and strong herbs have to be used in minute amounts, finely shredded. The basic principle is to combine a multitude of edible plant pieces without letting any one flavour dominate.

From each herb, take smaller or larger quantities, depending on their strength of flavour, tear or chop them finely and mix them well together with oil and vinegar, or keep them dry. Larger amounts of more conventional salading vegetables, such as shredded cabbage and grated celery, beet and carrot, can be added to dilute the herb portion and add a more crunchy texture. Add, mix and adjust to taste, as available, finely chopped: small amounts of rosemary, thyme, sage, marjoram, sweet cicely, summer savory, shungiku, coriander and fennel; large amounts of parsley, chervil, dill, French tarragon and basil; lots and lots and lots of chives and rocket; varying quantities to taste of mint, nasturtium leaves and flowers, purslane, Good King Henry, grated horseradish, land cress, citrus leaves, radicchio and alpine strawberries. Mix them up thoroughly, to be diluted with background saladings of: shredded carrot, grated red and green cabbage, shredded kohlrabi, chopped red and green pepper, celery, cucumber and gherkin bits, tender curly kale leaves, corn salad, claytonia and even lettuce, chicory, endive, almost any edible green, and baby peas. Then add pot marigold, day lily (*Hemerocallis*), pelargonium and shungiku petals; borage and rosemary flowers; and violet, pansy, bergamot and rose petals.

When ready to serve, top with sliced Gardener's Delight tomatoes and sprinkle with hull-less pumpkin, poppy, celery and sunflower seeds. I rarely use salad dressings on this, preferring to keep it dry and serve it in combination with a well-moistened dish such as taramasalata, hummus, egg mayonnaise and so on.

Rocket, chervil and dill, parsley, spring onions, lettuce and endive (*Eruca vesicaria, Anthriscus cerefolium, Anethum graveolens, Petroselinum, Allium, Lactuca sativa, Cichorium enidivia*)

These are among the most valuable of all home crops: with repeated sowings in pots, under cover and in the open ground, and more in winter in warmth, you can have them fresh all year round with no great difficulty. Sow rocket every fortnight and the others every month and you will never regret it; do not bother with old plants – pull them. With the latter three listed above, there are different varieties for sowing at different seasons; with the lettuce it is most economic to grow loose-leaf, cut-and-come-again varieties. Of course, it is a good idea to grow extra masses of dill in spring and summer for preserving in vinegar with cucumbers and gherkins.

Claytonia miner's lettuce, Valerianella corn salad

These are two leafy salad crops, both very good at growing in the cool conditions of late autumn and early spring, and under cover all winter through, providing masses of succulent leaves. Claytonia can also be boiled down, sieved and frozen as a spinach.

Spinaches (*Spinacia oleracea*)

These are grown just like salad crops, with repeated sowings in rich moist soil, and picked while still young and succulent. You can boil the washed leaves and small stems to a pulp, sieve and freeze in half-full plastic cups or small bags. To get cleaner leaves, it is worth planting small cell-grown plants through holes in plastic, cardboard or newspaper. There are different spinaches for early and late sowings, and other species, such as New Zealand, for drought conditions, all of which can be treated the same way to put leafy greens away for the rest of the year.

Pak choi and Chinese greens (*Brassica rapa*)

These are more vegetables than salad crops, but are grown more like the latter in much-enriched and moistened soil. They do better from summer and autumn sowings, and only a few varieties do not bolt if sown in spring. The late and winter crops do need cloches, or to be kept under cover, to prevent weather damage, and slugs are very attracted to them. However, they can give you cut after cut of succulent stems and leaves for stir-frying. The roots come again if the top is removed, giving a bonus crop. They could presumably be brined or turned into a Chinese sauerkraut, but their greatest value is in their freshness and crunchiness.

LEFT Saladings are most reliable started in cells under cover, then planted out.

Vegetables: roots, alliums, legumes, brassicas, curcubits, solanaceae, seeds, perennial

A lot of vegetables can have their season extended a bit if you sow early and late varieties, and many keep well in the ground or stored; these are barely worth storing by other means, except to bridge the empty gaps. In general, vegetables are a little more risky to preserve than fruits because of their lack of acidity or high sugar levels, and more moulds and rots attack them, which may make us sick. This means much greater care needs to be taken with bottling, and is why I prefer pickles and chutneys, where the extra preservative actions of vinegar and sugar add safety. Drying is relatively safe, and dried vegetables, packed in airtight boxes (and even frozen as well) should remain good for emergencies for decades.

ROOTS

Most of these are biennials, storing up energy this year to flower next. Bolting is their reaction to sudden tough conditions – they flower early, becoming useless to us – so keep them growing without check. For storing, a high dry-matter content and not bloated crops are preferable, so give them plenty of water early on, but not so much once they are three-parts grown – and never give them anything with an off flavour, such as rank manure water, especially towards maturity.

Carrots *(Daucus carota subsp. sativa)*

Highly nutritious, good for us and sweet, these can be had year round. With some simple protection and selected varieties, a few can even grow in winter. There is an immense variety, with a plethora of colour and shapes. There are even short stumpy ones for shallow soil or pots. They are easy about soil fertility and pH level, but don't use too fresh manure, which can cause distortion and fanging (when the roots break up into many little branches); indeed no manures or fertilisers should be applied before carrots are sown, and they should not follow peas or beans. I prefer to sow them after an onion crop into an undisturbed soil with only a sowing tilth made. Indeed carrots grow really well in deep pots – given space to swell sideways! They need a lot of water for the smaller forcing ones to be sweet and succulent, but once their roots are down the slower-growing ones can do well, even in mild droughts. They love seaweed sprays, and the main pest, the root fly, is simply kept off with fine meshed netting supported over the crop and held to the ground all round.

Varieties

There are the Nantes types and others, such as the classic 'Amsterdam Forcing', that are quick-growing and can be sown fairly close if the soil is rich and moist. A succession of a selection of these gives summer carrots outdoors; these will also provide the early and very late sorts for growing under cover in spring, autumn and winter. Then there are all sorts of divisions by shape and genetics, but basically the other group are the larger-growing ones that grow more slowly, take more space and usually store well.

Harvest

By covering with plastic and mulches you can store carrots in the ground or dig them and keep them in the root store – ideally, packed in slightly moist sand. Twist the leaves off when you're packing them, or even just picking them, as they bleed more if cut, it is said. However, oddly, I found some stored carrots were okay for a long time even though I'd accidentally cut the whole top off and sealed the end with wood ashes. Likewise a row of carrots about to bolt can be de-shouldered in the ground, covered with wood ashes and then sand and will keep for weeks more.

BELOW **Carrots can be grown in deep pots most successfully.**

carrot cake

Cream together 7 ounces (200g) butter and an equal amount of brown sugar until light and fluffy. Gradually beat in 3 eggs, lightly whisked, $\frac{1}{2}$ teaspoon or so of powdered cinnamon and a couple of drops of vanilla extract. Stir in 14 ounces (400g) finely grated carrots, a handful of raisins and 7 ounces (200g) self-raising flour. The mixture should be quite stiff. Spoon into a greased and lined cake tin and bake in a medium oven, 180°C/350°F/ gas mark 4, for about 50 minutes, until cooked through. Cool on a wire rack.

This makes a very moist, dense cake, best served with butter and jam and eaten with a fork

Do not just pull carrots, as their tops will come away; push a fork in vertically beside them – but a hand's thickness away – and lever ever so slightly, then pull and they will come more easily. Huge ones will be damaged by the tines if you're not careful where you place them. I have a two-tined (it once had four) fork just to dig and lever either side more accurately. Rub off excess soil, but wash only those you will use right away.

Preserving and use
Carrots can be sliced and dried, and in theory can be bottled. You can cube or slice them, blanch, cool and freeze them. But as they are available so easily all year round, why bother? They can be juiced – and the juice frozen and drunk promptly and with due care. The pulp left over can be made into carrot cake, and this frozen. Carrots are good as pieces in pickles and chutneys, and can be mashed with butter and this frozen for later. They make quite good little crisps – but burn easily if the oil is too hot. In theory, carrots make a strong wine, but it's not very palatable on its own, so combine it with raisins and oranges, beetroot or elderberry. Carrot seed is used in some liqueurs.

Turnips and swedes *(Brassica rapa/napus)*
Turnips are quick and can be grown much like salad crops in successional sowings almost year round with cloches or under cover in winter. The swede is a slower-growing turnip that matures in autumn; it will store till hard frosts come in the ground, but is safest removed to the root store before then. Twist the leaves off and pack them in moist sand. The young shoots and leaves of turnips that sprout in store can be eaten – they are quite a delicacy; those of turnips left in the ground are greener and stronger-tasting but still good. Small cubes of turnip or swede are often included in pickles and chutneys. Mashed buttered swede, if frozen, discolours but is okay. I suppose you could dry or bottle turnips, but I doubt even the biggest glut would ever be worth turning into the wine – though recipes are often given, as they are for carrots.

RIGHT **Pull carrots fresh as required; they can be had year round.**

Parsnips *(Pastinacea sativa)*

These roots are considered best after frosts have got at them, so are invariably left in the ground until required. Sow them normally early in spring – though some varieties such as 'Dagger' can be close sown and used more like carrots and then in small successional batches. Once they're mature, leave them standing; sometimes they'll need protecting against very hard frosts, simply so they can be dug. And if you want your parsnips early but with a frosted taste just dig them up, wash and stick them in the freezer overnight wrapped in several newspapers, then let them defrost for a day before cooking.

In theory, parsnips could be dried; they make good crisps and excellent chips: parboil them, chip and part-fry and freeze them to finish off later when required. Parsnips are as sweet as carrots and make a nicer wine – honest, give it a go! – especially when combined with apricot, peach or fig. Try it – after all, you never know.

Beetroots and chards *(Beta vulgaris)*

Beetroot comes in a range of shapes and even colours; the white is good and the yellow excellent. Essentially, chards and spinach beet are the leafier forms of the same plant as beetroot, and indeed the leaves of beetroot can be used as a spinach. With cloches and successional sowing of a selection of early and late good storers, you can have fresh beetroot year round. For sweet, tender beetroot, sow small batches regularly in a rich moist soil – the only worry is the birds, so keep them off. Pickle beetroot, however small, as they are all good. The skins will slip off easily after cooking.

Beetroots are invariably pickled, traditionally in sweet spiced malt vinegar, but I like the yellow 'Burpee's Golden' in spirit vinegar to keep the clear colour. They can be dried, but are better crisped. The part-cooked chips do not freeze as well as potato ones. Beetroot can be made into a jam, but is more often used in pickles and chutneys, and the colour is useful in many dishes. They make a red wine, their cousin the sugar beet an even stronger white. For wine, they combine well with elderberries, blackcurrants or loganberries.

OPPOSITE **Grow small to medium, not huge, beetroot, which can be woody.**

pickled beetroot

Pick and wash the beet, twist the leaves off and boil them with their skins on until you can easily push a blunt knife through them, then drain and cool. Slip the skins off as they cool, then slice the beet into a jar of malt or cider vinegar. See pages 62–63.

Some people add salt and spices, but with good beetroot they are superfluous

parsnip, beetroot, carrot and potato crisps

Take a few parsnips, carrots, potatoes and beetroots. Use firm, fresh vegetables for the best results. Peel and slice very thinly and uniformly as possible. Heat about a pint of sunflower oil in a deep-sided pan or wok. To test that the oil is the right temperature, drop in a small cube of bread, it should sizzle and turn golden brown. If the oil is not hot enough the crisps will be soggy.

Set up a wire rack on a tray lined with kitchen paper and begin frying each vegetable separately; a few at a time so as not to overcrowd the pan, as this will reduce the cooking temperature. Stir the vegetables with a slotted spoon to prevent sticking and remove to the rack to drain.

Pound a little salt with a tad of garlic and a morsel of onion, then mix this with more salt and some fresh ground pepper. Put the cooled crisps into a large bag with the salty flavouring and shake to coat them all lightly. Keep sealed if not eaten immediately. (The best potato for this is 'Record'.)

Celery and celeriac

Celery is not an easy crop to grow, requiring inordinately moist, extremely rich soil, but other than slugs it has few problems. It is normally started in warmth and planted out in spring for a summer and autumn crop, but it can be had fresh much of the year round if taken as closely-sown smallage, or leafy stalks, rather than big crunchy heads. Even self-blanching types benefit from having their heads wrapped to keep them dark, and if they are then covered over with insulation and a plastic sheet they can be held in situ for some months through winter. Do not forget to let a celery plant go to seed and then collect the seed, for it is an essential in so many savoury dishes, and in love potions.

Celeriac, grown similarly, is much easier; don't forget to pull off the oldest lower leaves as they start to wither, to encourage the stem base to swell. Store it just as you would cabbage, or roots, and use peeled and sliced or grated. Florence fennel is much like celery but with an aniseed taste; it needs to be grown quickly in moist rich soil, and is better from later summer sowings for use in the autumn. I have never tried to do much with this, but it seems suited for a Pernod-like liqueur, if that's to your taste.

Artichokes, Jerusalem and Chinese (Helianthus tuberoses)

These are similar to one another in having hard-to-peel irregular tubers, but the Jerusalem will grow anywhere, is tougher than old boots and gets taller than sunflowers, while the Chinese is squat and looks somewhat like lemon balm and is a tad tender. Either are best par-boiled, the skins slipped off and then fried. Be warned the Jerusalem causes wind! Both are best left in the ground until required; indeed they are often given permanent sites. Covering them with mulch and a plastic sheet will make them diggable in hard weather – but do put rodent traps in place first! I have never heard of anyone wishing to store these any other way, but I guess they could be dried or pickled… and, as mad as it sounds, there is even a home-made wine from them!

celery soup

Roughly chop two young heads of celery, a large onion and a couple of potatoes. Sauté in a little oil or butter, cover with stock and bring to the boil. Simmer until all the vegetables are soft and purée with a stick blender (or pass through a sieve, in which case thicken with cornflour mixed into a little milk). Season with salt and white pepper.

Serve piping hot with crusty bread and cheese

ALLIUMS

These are vital for almost every savoury dish; packed full of minerals they are also healthy. And, fortunately, they are relatively easy to grow and store. Very high in sulphur, they like a firm soil, following brassicas or sweet corn well, or preceding them with minimal cultivation (do not dig, but firm their bed). Use generous seaweed and wood-ash applications to ensure they store well.

Onions (*Allium cepa*)

Grow these in full sun. Spacing is important: far apart = big ones, close together = small. For pickling, and where you want hard small ones for long storage, sow them five seeds to a cell and plant out unthinned. Or plant shallot sets, as the only difference from true onion is that shallot sets multiply so need more space, and the flavour is milder. Sowing is cheap, but planting sets – small onions – is simpler. By sowing some in pots from late winter and planting these out, with later-sown batches following, and doing likewise with the sets, you will have small onions by early summer and big ones by midsummer, ripening with any heat to store well.

You shouldn't sow onions late, not even in late spring, as they won't grow to any size; if you do, these small bulbs are best used for re-setting the next year. You can, of course, sow some varieties of spring onion year round, for fresh, slightly bulbous onions. But for storing, get the seed or sets in as soon as possible each spring.

There is another window: autumn-sown sets or seed, especially Japanese varieties, started in mid-August come through the winter and swell earlier, giving bulb onions from late spring and weeks before the usual spring seed or sets. These are useful for that late-spring gap when the stored ones have run out, but they do not keep well so must be used or processed by mid-autumn.

When planting onion seedlings or sets, set them high, up on top of the soil not down in it; deep-grown onions have thick necks and do not store well. Indeed, put them on small ridges and, once they're established, remove the ridges, leaving them proud. Be careful not to push sets into the soil as this bruises the basal plate and they may not grow. A crop of weeds allowed to grow as the onions ripen and die down improves their storing, though they would be too detrimental any earlier.

Harvest

You can pull onions as needed, thinning as you go, but for the biggest crop they need to grow on until they die down in summer – their natural habit. It does more harm than good to bend their necks down to speed this up, as was once thought necessary. It is

ABOVE **Shallots and onions need dry, airy conditions to store well.**

more advantageous to push a spade underneath and sever the roots a few inches below the bulb, and better still to dig them carefully and dry them in a hot, dry, airy place, such as on the greenhouse staging in full sun. The better they dry down, the better they keep, and big ones don't keep as well as small ones. Do handle them gently, and if the basal root plate is damaged or any are bruised, use them straight away.

Preserving and use

Onions have to be kept in the air, and mild cold is no problem; even frost can touch them and they'll be fine. But any damp and they'll rot. So they are best laid on wire or plastic netting hammocks or trays hung in the eaves of airy sheds. They are safer in bulk when very well dried, when they can be bagged in nets. Tying them in bunches or strings is risky, though it looks cute. Ideally, peg them to wires in a dry roof space. In spring when the late storers sprout, do not throw them away but plant them together in a corner or a big pot. The young leaves and base can then be used as big spring onions or chopped for cooking as scallions.

onion marmalade

Finely slice and chop onions, then caramelise them with a little sunflower oil in a covered pan by heating slowly and stirring. Once they have started to brown, add half their weight of either concentrated apple juice or a mix of fifty-fifty red or whitecurrant juice and sugar. Simmer slowly until the onions are softening and breaking up (about 45 minutes), add a tad of salt and pepper, bring near to boil, then jar and seal immediately.

The commercial onion marmalades are often made with pomegranate juice, which you may like to try

leek and potato soup

Take a couple of large leeks and clean thoroughly to remove any grit. Chop roughly (reserving the green parts for stock) and sauté in butter until softened. Grate or finely chop a couple of peeled potatoes, add to the pan and cover with hot stock. (Home-made if possible, otherwise a good bouillon will do.) Simmer until all the vegetables are soft and broken down, season and serve. Alternatively pass through a sieve or liquidise, add some cream to taste, chill and serve garnished with some chopped chives.

cold leek appetiser

Boil clean leeks, whole except for leaves and roots, in a stock – preferably chicken – and let them cool in it. Drain, then marinate in white wine vinegar and chopped parsley. They can be frozen like this for later use. Eat with poppy seeded bread rolls and butter.

Onions can be dried very easily; the bigger rings of each slice just hang along a string so neatly. The smaller central core is better used fresh, or made into a wee pickled onion. I've smoked dried onion rings, and these were really good for adding to soups. Unless they are fried, freezing does not suit onions and they will, of course, taint everything else unless well sealed. However, they freeze better when made into ratatouille, curries, casseroles or other meals. And battered onion rings, part-fried, freeze well, though this isn't very economical on space.

Surprisingly, onions can be jammed – well, marmaladed is closer to it: you can make this sweet savoury pickle by caramelising onions with redcurrant juice and apple concentrate. If you were curious enough, you might try candied or crystallised onion rings. Onions make really good chutneys and sauces. If you're trying to get more out of your meat dishes, use your usual spices but apply them in a paste made by squidging onion through a garlic press. Believe me or not, there are recipes for onion wine – but I'm drawing the line before there! Pickling onions is, of course, the perfect processing method.

Pickled onions, shallots or garlic

Remove the dirt and dry outer skins from the onions, rinse well and cover with brine. Leave to soak for one day for garlic and shallots and two days for bigger onions. Drain and rinse the bulbs and slip off the next layer of tough skin. Pack into a jar with a bay leaf, a few whole peppercorns and a chilli, if you like, and cover with vinegar. Wine vinegar is best for delicate silver skins, cider vinegar for garlic, and malt vinegar for shallots and most onions. Dissolve a couple of spoonfuls of sugar in the vinegar if you like a sweet pickling marinade.

Garlic (*Allium sativum*)

Garlic needs no description. Put the offsets in finger deep in October or November and dig them the next July – before their leaves totally disappear, or you won't find them all. Any open sunny site suits them; bigger spacing and early planting give the best crops. Then it is all down to the drying, or they won't keep. Even more than onions, they must be kept dry!

Garlic can be dried – either as whole cloves or as slices – and then packed away in dry salt in small jars while still just supple. (The cloves can be oven-dried to wee biscuits, but then lack much flavour.) Dried garlic is very handy when the stored crop runs out in late spring – though once the stored ones sprout they can be potted up and then be used fresh, leaf and all. Garlic should not be frozen or used in anything frozen unless your seals are superb. But garlic does pickle magnificently, making really poky little bites.

Leeks (*Allium porrum*)

Unlike the other alliums, these like rankly overfed wet soil – and then they grow huge. They still like full sun, though, doing badly in shade. Leeks are an autumn and winter crop, tolerating almost all weather and growing in mild spells until they bolt in spring. The bolted stems can be left – the flowers are good for insects – and when dried make interesting flower arrangements and, if sprayed silver or gold, great Christmas-tree baubles. You can sow from very early in late winter under cover, in pots, and plant out later, and follow these with a succession of batches with the slower-maturing for the later use. As with onions, though, there is no point sowing once mid-spring is reached – unless you want to use them like spring onions. Another way is to cut back the flower stem; the leek will produce offsets, which can be replanted for another crop, as can the bulbils and seedlings formed in flower heads.

Harvest

Push a spade straight down on each side of a leek plant to sever the roots there before lifting. If you carefully dig around and sever the leek just above the base, this may heal over and proliferate loads of small leeklets for transplanting.

Preserving and use

Simply store leeks where they grow – although I also put some in containers, which is a good way to grow them, and these can be moved under cover for when hard frosts make the outdoor crop undiggable. Leeks can be dug, topped and tailed, then packed in trays and kept for some weeks in a root store. If you wash leeks, keep them upside-down so as not to drive silt into the leaf gaps.

Leeks can be sliced lengthwise into flat sheets which can be dried really easily. These can then be cut with scissors into shreds for soups and stews. As with onions and garlic, they are better made into freezer meals – say, leek and potato soup – rather than frozen on their own. Leeks are not much used in pickles, chutneys or sauces, nor (unsurprisingly) in liqueurs and love potions. However, they make fantastic cold appetisers – see opposite.

LEGUMES

These are valuable for garden fertility as well as for food. Fresh ones as green beans, peas or green pods do require a lot of keeping up with, though they are easy to grow. However, there is no simpler crop than legumes for drying – sow, grow and cut off the whole plant when the crop is ripe. As the roots are left to feed the soil, every spare patch should be filled with these.

Beans, broad (*Vicia faba*)

These are not as widely enjoyed as they ought to be, as they're often picked too big and old. Sow them in autumn and late winter to early spring for a succession of small, early summer crops. Later crops rarely do well. Pick off the tips once the flowers have appeared to stop the aphids becoming a problem. The young bean pods can be picked, cooked and eaten whole but are not recommended in quantity. Although the beans can be dried and used for winter soups and casseroles, they are better blanched and frozen. Those with thick skins can have these slipped off after blanching; the beans can then be turned into an excellent meatless pâté.

Beans, French, green (*Phaseolus vulgaris*)

The dwarf French beans are easy to grow once the soil has warmed up, so are often better started in pots and planted out. They need to be at least a foot apart each way! There are running versions that need canes and wider spacing, but then give immense yields. Any good soil with lime, well watered and in full sun, suits them. Very early crops can be had under cover; very late crops under cover will succumb to botrytis too easily to be worth it, though they are possible. With varieties good for early forcing, some quick croppers and some slower, and with successional sowings you can have French beans from late spring till late autumn. Then, although they can be dried, or bottled in brine, or even salted (see page 64), they are without doubt best blanched and frozen. With these beans it is very much a case of pick often and never leave one to swell its seeds as then future production is reduced.

TOP LEFT AND RIGHT Beans need topping and tailing. After boiling them for a few minutes they need dropping into cold water and rapid cooling.
BOTTOM LEFT AND RIGHT Beans must be drained well, then further dried on kitchen towel before freezing loose on oiled trays.

broad bean pâté

Cook 1 pound 10 ounces (750g) shelled broad beans in boiling, salted water for 5–6 minutes until tender, cool then slip off their grey skins. Sauté an onion, finely chopped, a small red and green pepper, de-seeded and finely chopped, in a little olive oil until softened. Add the broad beans, a tablespoon of tomato purée, a splash of water, a bay leaf and some summer savory. Season and simmer for a few minutes more. Remove the bay leaf and any savory stalks, liquidise the mix until smooth (or pass through a fine sieve), tip into a bowl and mix in 3 ounces (75g) breadcrumbs and 2 eggs, lightly whisked, and spoon into a pie dish. Dot with butter, cover with foil and bake in a medium oven for 40 minutes. Cool and serve with toast and/or salad.

Of course, for the dried haricot seeds, the plants are just left to ripen and wither. Almost any French-bean seed can be dried and then used as a haricot bean, but the small pencil-podded beans have small seeds with lots of skin. The true drying varieties such as the old 'Horsehead' or 'Brown Dutch' have big seeds with fairly thin skins. Wrap the drying tops loosely in a net curtain and tie them in airy roof spaces till dried, then pack the beans in tins. It is actually possible to dry the green beans: when they are at their very best and not at all seedy, thread them on strings and hang in very drying places. Given a night's soaking they cook up amazingly well.

Beans, runner *(Phaseolus coccineus)*

These are often popular where the French are not. They require more moisture and need pollination, so can be more difficult. They can be started off in pots in spring and planted out after the frosts. A very early crop can be had if you dig the roots at the end of summer, overwinter them like dahlia tubers and force them from early spring under cover. However, for bounteous success sow the seeds in situ in late May or early June and you will be giving away carrier bags full. Pick these often and pick them young and tender. Then de-string the stringy sorts, slice finely, blanch and freeze. They can be dried – ideally, finely sliced and lightly brined first. Or you can salt them; indeed runner beans are one of the few vegetables still commonly preserved this way. And, although it is not commonly done, I have put the dried bean seeds, well soaked and boiled, in winter casseroles without complaint. The variety 'Csar', a white-seeded one, can be dried and used exactly as butter beans.

Beans, other

There are an awful lot of beans in the world. Most of them have poisonous foliage, and some beans must be cooked for long enough to make them safe. Almost all of them can have their seeds dried to be reconstituted and boiled later, but only a few are safe to eat as the pods; those that are can usually be blanched and frozen if you want to save a surplus. Soya beans have a whole foody world of their own! However, the current varieties are extremely difficult to grow well in temperate climates such as in the UK.

Peas *(Pisum sativum)*

These little green pearls are so wonderful freshly steamed in their pods that to eat them any other way seems hollow. However, as they are still good when frozen, pick them often and young and

LEFT A small crop of French beans can be had really early in a big pot under cover.

blanch and freeze as many as you can. The earliest outdoor crops can be chanced from late winter, but sow every week or so, and re-sow missing batches as you cannot have too many. Then watch them like a hawk, as they soon go over and become tough.

The mangetout edible podded peas can be blanched and frozen, as can the more succulent sugar-snap varieties. The former have strings that need removing. Petits pois are small and very sweet and require the least blanching; indeed they can be frozen without being blanched as long as you use them within a few months. It is no good blanching and freezing tough peas; they do not improve. Better to leave them on the vine to dry and then they can be collected for winter use – not as themselves in bulk but soaked overnight and added to soups and casseroles. Peas can be bottled in hot sweet brine, but need pressure cooking for safe storage.

BRASSICAS

All of these health-giving veggies require a rich, moist, limey soil – preferably in full sun – and are sown usually in spring, though some can be sown in midsummer to overwinter. They are all either sown in a seedbed and moved on or, better, sown singly in cells or pots and planted out, with protection from birds and other pests. The use of fleece is highly recommended. Using excessive fertiliser, especially muck, will give rank flavours and less storage ability. Brassicas benefit as much from wood ashes and lime, and love seaweed sprays and drenches.

Cabbages, kohls and kales (*Brassica oleracea var. capitata, Brassoca olereacea* and *Brassica olereacea Acephela* Group)

These can be had either fresh or stored every day of the year – from overwintered pointed-head spring cabbages through the dense coleslaw ball-heads of summer and autumn to the crinkly-leaved savoys of winter. There are varieties for sowing and harvesting early, or late, and specifically for storing, such as the Holland late whites. There is a huge number of varieties, changing rapidly, and now some that are clubroot-resistant for those growing on old infested sites. If you use fine netting or fleece protection, most pests can be kept off – save slugs: use traps, or risk them getting in the heads. Petroleum jelly smeared around the stem and dusted with soot or salt stops them climbing up. Once the heads are full size, you do not need to take the whole thing; just take a sloping slice off for what you need, and cover the wound with clingfilm – the rest will keep better on its roots than in the fridge. When you

RIGHT **Cabbage can be troubled but is still a reliable crop.**

cauliflower cheese

Wash a whole cauliflower making sure any foreign bodies are extricated (immersing it in salty water will do the trick). Place it in a large saucepan the with just enough water to cover the bottom of the pan and bring to the boil so the stalk is well cooked and the head steamed – about 15 minutes, then drain and place in a heated casserole dish. Meanwhile make a cheese sauce by boiling milk, adding this to cornflour and fresh ground white pepper, mixed with a little water in a bowl, about 2–3 tablespoonfuls to each pint (600ml) of milk depending how thick you want it. Return to the heat and, stirring constantly, allow it to thicken, then add a generous portion of grated cheese. Pour the cheese sauce over the cauliflower, top with more cheese and a sprinkling of smoked paprika and bake in a hot oven until golden brown.

have taken the head, cut a cross in the stem and remove most of the leaves and you will often get a new crop of small, softer heads.

The plants can be lifted, roots and all, and ideally hung upside-down in a trench, tied between two wooden supports and covered over with a plastic sheet and mulches, and will keep for months. Or you can just chop the heads off and stack them in boxes or net bags in a root store. The red keep as well as the green. If slugs have got in, give them a good coating of salt; this stops them moving from damaged to fresh places. As cabbage is so easily had year round, the only common way of preserving it is the sauerkraut route (see page 64).

Kohl rabi is grown just like cabbage, but it is the swollen stem that is eaten, either raw or cooked. They can be stored just like roots. Kales are effectively very hardy, loose-leafed cabbages and are usually left in the ground all winter for use fresh picked. They can be deep-fried to make seaweed – delicious.

Coleslaw variations

Coarsely grate a quarter of a firm white cabbage. Mix this with a large peeled carrot, a cored dessert apple, both finely grated and a small onion, very finely diced. Mix in a bowl with mayonnaise or salad cream, season and garnish with chopped chives. You can make Kohlslaw by replacing the cabbage with kohl rabi. You might like to add grated celery to the mix, finely diced red/green peppers, cooked sweet corn kernels or perhaps peas or sultanas. For making dinner parties go with a bang dilute the mayonnaise with white rum, but do warn your guests!

Cauliflower and broccolis (Brassica oleracea Botrytis and Cymosa Group)

Caulis are summer and autumn heading, and broccolis winter and spring heading. Like cabbages, the main problems are kept away by fleece or fine net. One way to get rid of infestations of slugs, aphids and caterpillars is to immerse the head in brine and then, once the critters have quit, drain, rinse and use or process. The heads do not grow again, and once cut they wither quickly, though the whole plant can be kept for weeks in the cool and dark. When the white curd sees the light it turns yellow, so break halfway through leaves and bend them to cover the curd over. Pick in the early morning for maximum crispness. Cauliflower florets can be blanched and frozen, or made into cauliflower cheese and frozen. It can also be brined and vinegared and added to mixed pickles.

bubble and squeak

Although this can be made with a variety of leftover vegetables, my local dish always includes Brussels sprouts and potatoes. These are mashed together with a very finely sliced onion, seasoned and formed into little patties. Shallow-fry in lard or sunflower oil over a medium heat until brown and crispy. Sprinkle with salt.

Brussels sprouts (*Brassica oleracea* Gemmifera group)
These are usually midwinter crops, though with early sowings you can have them by mid-autumn if you want. The main crop are for Christmas-time, and some will stand on until spring. Their soil needs to be rich and very firm; and bury the transplants a tad deeper than with other brassicas. In windy areas, tie three plants together as self-supporting tripods. To get the buds to swell sooner, take the top out of the plant – you can boil it as greens. Once off the stem they go off more quickly than if the whole stem is taken. Stems, less leaves, can be stored for several weeks without the sprouts suffering. They taste better once frosted, so early pickings are best after a night in the freezer. They can be blanched and frozen, but not very well; they freeze better as bubble and squeak.

CUCURBITS
This useful family are all tender, and are best started individually in pots in the warm, then hardened off and planted out as the weather warms up. They all love rich, moist soil, and are all promiscuous and will cross if different varieties are grown; this can occasionally affect the crop, as well as the future seed. They often do not make female flowers if too hot. And most are vigorous

ramblers, though a few more compact sorts may be available.

Marrows, courgettes and zucchini (Cucurbita)
These are all essentially the same thing, the difference being that marrows were traditionally grown for size and do not store long past harvest festival. Courgettes and zucchini are baby marrows, and if continually taken when small and then continually replaced they can be had in tremendous numbers from one plant. They can be dried – I've even smoked them dry; bottling them is too fiddly. I do not find they are very good frozen, even if blanched first – but if they are sliced and part-fried they can be packed in the oil and frozen. Or they can be incorporated into ratatouilles and other dishes for freezing. The flowers are also edible, and good for stuffing with savoury or sweet delights. A marrow can be converted into a potent wine: hang it in a net, remove the top, pour in a fermenting mixture of wine yeast in apple juice and ginger, then replace the top. Keep it in a warm place to let it ferment; then, after a month, make a pinhole in the bottom and drain the liquor out, measure it and add another two pounds of sugar per gallon (1kg per 5 litres). Leave this to ferment in a demijohn till finished, then decant and bottle.

FAR LEFT Winter storing squash need a good bit of stalk left to help them keep.

LEFT Nipping the top out of Brussel sprout plants helps the sprouts swell.

stuffed courgette flowers

Pick just newly opened flowers. Remove the inner stamen, being very careful not to damage the petals. Make a savoury filling by frying a small chopped onion, with 12 ounces (350g) minced pork, a slosh of white wine, a tablespoon tomato purée, a grated apple, a little chopped sage and some stock, just to cover. Cook for about half an hour until reduced and tasty, cool slightly and add a handful of bread-crumbs. Carefully stuff the flowers with the mix and place into a baking dish.

Prepare a tomato sauce by simmering peeled, de-seeded ripe tomatoes with a small chopped onion, lightly fried with a clove of garlic in olive oil, until thick and glossy. Add some oregano, seasoning and a pinch of sugar. Spoon this sauce around and over the flowers and bake in a medium oven for half an hour.

Courgette flowers are so easy to fill – they can be used in place of vine leaves or nori seaweed for wrapping fillings or rice

baked pumpkin or squash

To prepare the pumpkin, remove the lids and scrape out the seeds. Place into a baking dish, season and drizzle with olive oil. Roast for 20 minutes or so in a medium oven, whilst you prepare the filling.

Make a forcemeat with minced meat or good sausage meat, about a pound (450g) – or you could use cheese. Add a chopped onion, some thyme or sage and fry all together in olive oil until lightly browned. Add a slug of wine if you like. Season well and add a handful of breadcrumbs to absorb some of the juices. Spoon the mix into the cavity of the pumpkins, replace the lids and return to the oven for another 20–30 minutes until the squashes are soft and browning around the edges.

The small winter-storing squashes are much tastier to use here than the larger Halloween varieties which tend to be rather watery and lacking in flavour

Pumpkins and squashes (*Curcubita maxima/pepo*)

The summer soft-skinned ones keep no better than marrows and must be used quickly. The winter-storing varieties have thick skins, and some can keep over a year; these should not be neglected as a fresh stored vegetable, as they can be used in both sweet and savoury manners. They keep best suspended in soft nets or laid on shredded newspaper in an airy frost-free place. It is important to let them ripen on the vines and to detach them with a good length of stem. The Hubbards and blue varieties such as 'Crown Prince' seem to be the longest keepers – I had one still edible for the second Christmas after the autumn it ripened!

Pumpkins can be baked and the pulp frozen or cooked in other dishes. With the sweeter ones some people even make jams, often flavoured with ginger and lemon or cinnamon. An additional bonus is the seeds; although most have a tough case, this can be removed after the dried seeds have been toasted with some salt. Or the hull-less varieties can be grown; these have an edible flesh as usual, but also the seeds have a thin skin that is easily washed off. Once thoroughly dried, the seeds will store for some years.

Cucumbers and gherkins (*Cucumis sativus*)

Grown in the same way as the other outdoor cucurbits, these can be picked small and pickled. There are some differences between ridge outdoor cucumbers and gherkins, but their small fruits are almost interchangeable, once brined and pickled. The greenhouse cucumbers are a fresh salad crop, and if you sow in heat under cover in the New Year, you can be eating cucumbers from Easter. As the plants crop hugely if well fed, they can give an enormous surplus, but other than pickling them there is little you can use them for – face packs, maybe. The tips of healthy plants can be layered to start new healthy cropping plants to replace the older worn-out ones, and with some heat you can get crops into early winter, but you will probably lose the plants in the cold dark nights.

Melons and watermelons (*Cucumbia melo* and *Citrullis lanatus/vulgaris*)

In cold years, greenhouse crops of these are the only ones in the UK. Indeed, most years it is not worth growing them without some cover and without starting them off in the warm. I lay plastic sheets down to warm the soil, with a clear plastic tent over the top, and it is not until the soil underneath is warm at night that I plant out. Then I get crops. It is more often sensible to grow these in big pots under cover, with a bit of extra warmth. In every case it is better to limit the number of fruits set so that you get fewer,

ABOVE Cucumbers are not difficult under cover and crop heartily.

bigger fruits with less waste on seeds and skin. I've found that only the earliest flowers ever need pollinating manually; later in the year insects abound. Melon fruits need to be suspended in a bag or rested on some soft, warm, dry material, such as expanded polystyrene or balsa wood, to stop them dropping and rolling away, as melons are best eaten when they fall away from their stalk – you will see the cracking start. Watermelons get a hollow sound when tapped if they are ready.

Fresh melons and watermelons will not store very well; they are best taken once fully ripe and eaten warm for the melon and chilled for the watermelon. Neither freezes nor dries satisfactorily. Both can be turned into rather runny jam, though the melon loses much of its fine flavour in the process; they are best chunked and sugared overnight – this reduces the fruits to smaller, chewier pieces. Melon can be candied or crystallised, or bottled in syrup or pear concentrate. Watermelon is so juicy that either of these is difficult, so it's best juiced and frozen – though it will benefit from being mixed with something tangier such as ginger, lemon or apricot.

piccalilli

Piccalilli is a glorious mixture of small pieces of courgette, cucumber, cauliflower florets, small onions ('Paris Silverskin'), sometimes with tiny green tomatoes, raisins or sliced green beans and even cubes of swede and turnip; all floating in a sweet (or spicy) mustard sauce. Not all these crops are going to be available to harvest the same week, no matter how clever you are. So when each is available, brine it overnight in a pound of salt per gallon of water (500g per 5 litres), drain it, wash it and pickle it in vinegar. Then leave this to await the others so that all can be mixed together in the mustard sauce and be potted and bottled. Heat the pickled pieces in – and then strain them of – their vinegar, which is made up to roughly two pints for every four pounds of pieces (1 litre for every 2kg). Add the spices – say half an ounce (15g) each of fresh ginger, dried turmeric and yellow mustard powder and up to a half-pound (225g) of sugar, depending on how sweet you like it. Re-boil the vinegar and stir in about an ounce (30g) of cornflour – pre-mixed with some of the vinegar – until it thickens. Then add the pieces back, bring back to the boil, then pot and bottle it. (If you like you can reduce the sugar and add chilli or more ginger instead.)

pickled gherkins

After picking your gherkins or small cucumbers, wash them and brine them overnight. Then drain, wash and cover them in hot cider vinegar and leave to cool. Drain again, reheat the vinegar and pour it over them again the next day, and so on, till they turn a brighter green. Pack them in jars of cider vinegar with dill (rather than spices) as flavouring. Small to medium-size cucumbers can also be brined and preserved in sweetened spirit vinegar and are especially tasty with spices, such as chilli, added.

SOLANACEAE

This family of plants nearly all have poisonous leaves and other parts, and although they are almost all fruits they are considered part of the vegetable garden. Furthermore, although some may succeed in warm gardens in good summers, most need to be in a greenhouse or at least under a cloche or cold frame. They all need to be started off early in the year, ideally in individual pots in warmth, and then potted on and planted out as soon as the soil is warm enough – preferably with extra protection. They also can do well in pots, if given enough water.

Tomatoes *(Lycopersicum lycopersicum)*

These are one of the most commonly grown crops – almost all gardeners have their own favourite. It is possible to have fresh tomatoes from late spring till midwinter – and although that gap is fillable if you have extra heat and light, it is barely worth the effort. If you must, try 'Sub-Arctic Plenty'. The earliest crops come from fast varieties started off in midwinter in the warm and kept in

OPPOSITE It's easy to grow your own tomato plants under cover
BELOW Grow tasty tomatoes such as the Brandywine series

pots up on frost-free staging. I de-head one leaf after the first flower truss to get an even more rapid crop. The next fruits come from less severely treated plants, then from plants in the greenhouse border and eventually outdoors. These last plants for outdoors do not need to be sown before early spring as they soon make up.

If you are after flavour rather than weight, in pots they need careful frequent watering and very light but regular feeding. In the soil, just give them enough water to keep them from wilting. I do not like growing them in big pots – or worse, bags – but if you must, make sure they're really big and with some form of easy or automatic watering, as otherwise you will get many fruits with hard brown corky bottoms. (Hard green corky tops mean they are getting too hot.) Generally, people overfeed and over-water and get bigger crops of tasteless red balls.

Do nip out side-shoots – these can be potted up to make extra, and very good squat, plants. To get the first flowers to set, use a brush; to get the first to ripen, put banana skins or dandelion leaves near them. Do not leave ripe fruits on the vines as this dissuades more from setting. Outdoors, if blight is threatening gather all the crop you can before it is spoilt. 'Ferline', 'Legend', 'San Marzano' and 'Histon Cropper' seem the most resistant so far (that is, they take longest to die).

Varieties

The small cherry tomatoes, especially 'Gardener's Delight', 'Sungold' and 'Sakura', are always popular. They're quick to crop and they do indoors and out – but, for processing, there are a lot of pips and skins. I prefer these fresh, and if a surplus needs storing I freeze them whole and de-skin them when they're thawing. The usual standard-size tomatoes, such as the classic 'Ailsa Craig', also come in a wide range of colours and flavours. The Marmande series and Beefsteaks are capable of producing huge tomatoes BUT ONLY IF you limit them to one per truss, and no more than two trusses to a plant at a time. The Brandywine series are fantastically well flavoured but a miffy bunch at best – still, they are worth growing under glass for the tasty huge fruits. The plum-shaped tomatoes, such as 'San Marazano' and the Roma series, are only for cooking and have no flavour till heated, when they become really tasty. With their higher dry matter they are the best for processing by most means, so you might want to concentrate on growing more of these.

Harvest

Pick tomatoes as they turn red; leaving them on longer reduces yields, although for drying they can be left to hang. They will keep in a fridge for weeks, but any surplus are best used rather than left to go old and wrinkled or rot. Green ones can be eaten once they are full size and are often preferred for jams, chutneys and pickles – the small cherry ones especially so. At the end of summer and when wet or frost starts to ruin the plants, pull them up, root and all, and hang them upside-down in a dry place; the fruits will continue to ripen for weeks and months. They must be frost-free, and the warmer they are, the faster they redden. Some keep green tomatoes in a padded kitchen drawer, ripening them up slowly or putting them on a sunny, warm windowsill to finish them quickly.

Preserving and use

Tomatoes can be dried; some may dry up of their own accord – but these will not be nice if they went rotten first, which is rather their way. There are some varieties bred for drying, though all can be dried; it is much a question of flavour. They need to be split before drying, and afterwards are best packed in herbed and garlicked oil. Tomatoes mould faster than most fruits when drying so, without fierce sun, I find that oven drying the halved fruits on trays is the only workable method. Tomatoes pre-dried this way can then be smoke-dried; this helps stop them moulding so they can be stored.

Freezing tomatoes is easy: wipe them, pop them in a freezer bag and freeze. When you want them, plunge each one in hot water and the skin will slip off. They take less space if reduced to juice or purée first. There are even hand machines, from Italian shops, that you turn to strip out the seeds and skins and some of the juice, leaving you with the important fleshy part to freeze or process.

Tomatoes are easy to bottle fairly safely, packed in brine, but are so easy to freeze that this has to be the first choice. They are fine when processed into frozen meals, especially ratatouille and pasta sauces. Maybe, unsurprisingly, tomato jams are made – or often the jellies, less the annoying skins and seeds. The golden varieties such as 'Golden Sunrise' make a beautiful jelly, especially if you add a bit of tartness with lemon/other citrus/whitecurrant juice.

But it is with pickles, chutneys and sauces that tomatoes prove most useful. They combine well with apples and onions to form a good base to accompany almost any other flavour and texture. Not really considered much use for wine or liqueurs, the tomato was, strangely, once associated with love potions.

green tomato chutney

Chop green tomatoes, taking care to make sure the skin is well divided, into smallish pieces, add a quarter their weight of peeled and cored apple, well chopped, and a quarter their weight of onions, very well chopped. Cover these with vinegar (cider is best though some may prefer malt) and simmer slowly and gently. Various spices may be added to taste, but I prefer a blend of powdered ginger, ground mustard, fresh ground white pepper and crushed garlic. Some may like to substitute curry powder or even chillies. Once the pieces are soft enough to be breaking down, add salt to taste and half the tomatoes' weight of sugar, white for a clean green chutney, Demerara or brown for a darker one, and continue to simmer till thick, then jar and seal. Allow a couple of months to mature before using.

spaghetti polognese

I was once making spaghetti bolog-
nese for a friend who does not eat red
meat, so I substituted minced chicken.
However, I felt it was lacking in
flavour so I upped the herbs and added
home-made sun-dried tomatoes. The
result was simply delicious.

Heat a tablespoon of oil in a pan and
cook a minced or finely chopped onion
and some garlic until softened.
Remove to a plate whilst you cook
the mince. Heat a little more oil and
thoroughly brown about a pound
(450g) of minced chicken. Add the
onion back to the pan with some
oregano, paprika, powdered ginger, a
bay leaf and some chopped basil. Add
a glass of red wine, a pound (450g) of
peeled, de-seeded tomatoes, roughly
chopped, 6 ounces (150g) chopped
marinated sun-dried tomatoes and half
a pint (300ml) of stock Bring to the
boil, and simmer gently for 45 minutes
to an hour. Top up with more stock if it
begins to catch. Cook some spaghetti,
stir through the sauce and serve.

Sweet peppers (Capsicum spp.)

Very high in anthocyanins and vitamins, as well as tasty and crunchy, these come in many colours and shapes. All are summer and autumn crops; even with heat it is hard to keep them growing in winter, and starting in early spring you will be lucky to get the first fruits by early summer. Remarkably easy to grow and crop – easier than tomatoes – they need an even better summer than tomatoes to do well outdoors. Large-fruited sorts may need staking. They will crop well in a large pot – even better in the ground, of course. Watch out for slugs holing the fruits.

Harvest

Green ones are edible (though they make some people prone to wind); as they ripen they change colour, usually to red but some to orange, yellow or blackish purple. Fresh, they keep in the frdige for a week or two but then need drying or freezing. I cut them into rings to string up and dry, and freeze all the offcuts as chunky bits. If you grill the pepper or attack it with a small blowtorch you can char the skin off, leaving the tasty smoky flesh ready to use in all sorts of dishes. They can be smoked dry and are then good in casseroles and stews. They can also be pickled, either on their own or, more often, as small bits in with other ingredients.

Chilli peppers

Grown in much the same way as sweet peppers and tomatoes, these come in even more colours and shapes and can be very, very productive. They can also vary in heat and taste by an astonishing degree. Be very careful picking and handling these. They dry easily and can be pickled or turned into the most fiery of sauces. I preserve habaneros until I want them for sauce by pricking them and then immersing them in spirit vinegar.

Aubergines (Solanum melongena)

Aubergines are useful for adding texture to sloppy dishes, and absorb whatever oils and flavours they are immersed in. As themselves they are remarkably bland and unappetising, even chargrilled. They are grown much the same as tomatoes, but rarely do aubergines succeed outdoors. Under cover they are not difficult, though do be careful of the small spines on the stems of the fruits.

OPPOSITE Chilli peppers are easy to grow and store well dried.

stuffed peppers

Prepare a savoury mince mixture as for the courgette flowers or stuffed squash (see pages 150–151). Any meat will do really, depending on your preference, or make a vegetable mix with whatever you have to hand, again binding with a handful of breadcrumbs. Stuff large ripe tomatoes or peppers with the mixture, drizzle with olive oil and bake in a medium oven. The tomatoes will take about half an hour, no longer or they will collapse, and the peppers slightly longer – 45 minutes to an hour until charring around the edges. In both cases, add a couple of slices of hard cheese to the top of each vegetable for the last 15 minutes until golden and bubbling.

ratatouille

Cut 2 aubergines into chunks. Place in a colander and sprinkle with salt. Set aside to drain then rinse and pat dry with kitchen paper. Slice 2 onions, 2 courgettes and deseed and slice a red and green pepper. In a large pan, fry each vegetable in olive oil until softened and golden; remove to a bowl whilst you fry the next. Add a couple of crushed garlic cloves to the pan, cook for a minute or two then return all the vegetables together with a sprig of thyme, rosemary and summer savory. In a separate pan, make some fresh tomato sauce: sauté a small chopped onion with a clove or two of garlic in some olive oil. Add a pound and a half (700g) ripe tomatoes, peeled and de-seeded. Turn the heat up and cook until the tomatoes collapse. Add to the vegetables with a bay leaf and a heaped tablespoon of tomato purée and simmer very slowly for 45 minutes or so until all the vegetables are meltingly soft. Season well and serve with toasted bread or croûtons.

For preserving, they are best peeled, salted and then cooked in oil and frozen for later use or combined into frozen meals. I imagine they could be dried, or pickled – but why? Amazingly they've escaped the notice of amateur wine-makers.

Physalis

This is a very valuable group of three tender tomato relatives. The most commonly known is the Cape gooseberry, *Physalis peruviana*. This is seen in the fruit section with papery lanterns containing golden balls, which are sweet and acid, somewhat like citrus. These can be had in autumn and winter from a spring sowing, and if the parent is overwintered or cuttings are taken in autumn, they crop earlier the following year, in summer. The fruits drop when ripe and lie under the plant to be gathered; if dry they will keep for many months, eventually drying to still-edible little raisins, in their paper cases. Almost immune to pests and diseases, this somewhat vigorous plant is really worth growing for these tasty, healthy fruits and will suffer the shadier greenhouse side. Best eaten fresh, the fruits can be made into a tasty jam-cum-jelly.

Demanding of more light and warmth is the tomatillo, *P. ixocarpa,* which has a bigger, green or purple fruit, still in a husk, and more like a tomato. These fruits can be used as tomatoes, in salsa dishes and to make jams. The ground cherry, *P. pruinosa*, is smaller and hardier and can be grown outdoors, though it does better under cover. This produces hundreds of smaller, greenish pineapple-flavoured fruits in tiny paper lanterns which keep for months and also make really good jam.

Potatoes *(Solanum tuberosum)*

The main food crop for many gardeners. There is a huge number of varieties and they come as earlies, second earlies, main crop and late main crops. This really means very quick to crop, or slower. Or, to be truthful, quick with small yields, slow with fair yields or very slow with the best yields. If all are sown or planted at the same time as small sets in late winter to early spring, the earlies will start to crop in June, the second earlies in July and the main crop in August, with the late main crops needing to be still growing into September to reach their full potential. Any sort can be stored, but obviously those dug first in the year need to be used first. The lates are better to store and most keep well anyway, unless blight is a problem – this makes lates difficult and you may need to rely more on high-yielding second earlies to store if the main crop and lates keep failing.

For new potatoes, with the early varieties you want lots of small

OPPOSITE **You can fry aubergines for freezing.**

potatoes quickly, so leave all the shoots on the sets and plant them close together – and it is worth chitting them before you plant them, which means starting the sets growing in a frost-free light place before they go in the ground. Put them in egg trays with their rose end – many eyes – uppermost. Later plant them that way up.

For main-crop and late storing potatoes you want fewer, bigger tubers, so these are not chitted first as this reduces the yields. Plant these as early as earlies but reduce the roots, or eyes, to three at the rose end and plant the sets with them uppermost and covered with soft soil. Plant these deeper and further apart than earlies.

You can plant earlies earlier in late winter in soil pre-warmed under cloches or plastic sheets, giving crops in May. But if you plant sets in big pots from Christmas on, and grow the plants somewhere cool, light and frost-free, you'll be eating new potatoes from Easter. 'Rocket' is currently one of the best for this sort of forcing, giving relatively good yields. You can also put earlies in late, as they crop in only three months; so they can be planted in March, and indeed every month up till July when they may still

just catch a crop outdoors. But even surer is to plant them in big pots in August from chilled sets you saved from spring and grow them under cover; then you have real new potatoes for winter.

Potatoes forced with too much manure or fertiliser break up and turn black when they are cooked; those overfed or over-watered do not keep well. They are best given plenty of wood ashes, comfrey liquid or leaves and seaweed sprays, and watered generously initially. One huge watering when any flowers appear improves the crop immensely. Remove all flowers and seed pods. Use every slug trap in the book, as damaged spuds store badly.

Varieties

These are difficult to recommend as there are so many, they taste different on different soils and people like different sorts. Most earlies are waxy, stay firm when cooked and are often called salad varieties. Many of the main and lates are mealy and break up powdery when cooked and are better for mash. My commonest plantings are 'Epicure', 'Sutton's Foremost' and 'Rocket', three good earlies. 'Charlotte' and 'Ratte' are good for salads. 'Pink Fir Apple' is a long-keeping old-time odd-shaped waxy one. 'Arran Victory' is a high-yielding late main crop good for mash, 'King Edward' another. 'Record' is best for crisps, 'Russet Burbank' and 'Golden Wonder' great for roasting. 'Rooster' and 'Lady Balfour' are good bakers. Grow 'Majestic', 'Cosmo', 'Fianna' and 'Valor' for chips and the 'Sarpo' blight-resistant sorts for a safety net.

OPPOSITE **It's always like digging for buried treasure.**

potato chips

Chips are a very personal thing, some like them big and fat and soggy, others like them thin and crisp. Personally I like them big, crispy and lightly browned on the outside and soft and creamy in the middle. The choice of potatoes is crucial, I rate 'Cosmos', 'Lady Balfour' and 'King Edward' as my favourites, 'Record' makes good ones with least oil absorbed. The oil is also crucial; olive oil is best but not all like the flavour, sunflower or corn oil is next, at all costs avoid cheap, blended or old frying oil. Lard makes good chips but with a greasy overtone, which some enjoy, and beef dripping makes them more of a meal with its own contribution to the taste. In any case, bring the potatoes into the warm well beforehand, peel and slice into chips and lay them on a cloth so their surfaces dry; you may wish to dip them in salted water to stop them browning in the air (which is not important), but drying their surfaces stops the oil spitting when they are added. Heat the oil to almost smoking, testing it by trying one chip on a fork, if it sizzles and bubbles then the oil is hot enough. Add the chips carefully! Stir to make sure none are sticking to the bottom or to each other and immediately reduce the heat. Keep them frying until the bubbling reduces and they all start to float on the surface, then increase the heat to a maximum to puff them up. Remove from the oil into a metal sieve placed in a saucepan to drain off any excess oil or lay them on kitchen paper. Add salt and pepper, and maybe malt vinegar, to taste. If you want them soggy, then cook long and slow, if you want them crispier, then make them slimmer and cook faster and hotter.

potato dauphinoise

Take about 2 pounds (900g) waxy potatoes, peeled and thinly sliced. Place in a pan and cover with a pint (600ml) milk or cream. Season, bring to the boil and simmer for 3-4 minutes. Butter a gratin dish and rub with a cut garlic clove. Spoon in the potatoes, smoothing out the surface as evenly as possible. Top with a mix of breadcrumbs and a generous sprinkling of grated cheese: I like to use a mix of Emmental, Gruyère and Parmesan. Bake in a medium oven, 180°C/350°F gas mark 4, covered with foil for the first half an hour, until the potatoes are completely cooked and the topping deeply golden, about 1¼ hours.

Top with a mix of breadcrumbs and a generous sprinkling of grated cheese: I like to use a mix of Emmental, Gruyère and Parmesan

Harvest

Cut down the haulm if blighted; otherwise leave it to die naturally. Dig the spuds on a dry day – sunny and windy, preferably; they will lie around the base of the stem, so dig them out carefully, gently rub off excess dirt and lay them to dry on sheets or similar. Once they are all up and have dried for an hour or two, select the perfect and best for long-term storage and put these aside in paper sacks, or on trays, in a cool, dark, dry place to cure for a week or so. Select the greened and damaged, but good ones, for sets for next year. Then use or process the rest as soon as possible, destroying any nasty ones.

Most potatoes kept in a store as suggested on pages 28–31 will keep fine till late winter. Then, as well as shrivelling if too dry, they will sprout. This can be delayed by rubbing out the first attempts and by chilling the store. An easy way is to leave it open at night – not on bitterly cold ones, though, as frozen spuds taste sweet – or to defrost frozen bottles of water in there. It is very advisable to put slug traps amongst your stored spuds. In the absence of a store they can be kept in any cool, dark, dry, rodent-free place; just do not bring them into the kitchen or the light until needed, as they pick up taints, wither and turn green and poisonous – even when left in the vegetable rack for just a few days.

Other than the usual storing, it is possible to slice potatoes thinly and dry them, though they tend to go black even if dipped in salt water. New potatoes can be bottled, but this is not recommended without pressure sterilising. They do not freeze well raw or mashed (they go browny black), but new potatoes three-quarters cooked, with mint, heavily buttered, cooled and packed in bags, can be frozen and will keep till your midwinter feast. Best of all is to part-fry potato chips, cool and open-freeze them, then bag them. Do not fully fry them. On defrosting they can be fried, or oven-baked, to finish them off. Potatoes can be fermented to a vile brew which, if legal, is better distilled to make vodka than drunk.

Sweet potatoes (*Ipomoea batatas*)

These are completely different from potatoes in many ways. They are grown from slips – best forced off a supermarket tuber – in late winter with some heat, then potted up and grown on under cover. They can be planted outdoors for a poor crop; the best are grown under cover in big tubs or bags of compost which can give them the required longer growing season. The haulm needs to be tied up in the light; it is a waste of energy to let it root on the ground – which it will do wherever it can touch it. Unlike those of potatoes, the roots do not become poisonous if they see light and turn green, but this is still not desirable. The plants need heavy watering and weekly feeding, and can give very good crops. Once dug, they must be used within a week or two as they soon rot. They can be heat-treated to keep longer; several hours in a warm open oven slowly cures them. They keep better warmer and drier than 'ordinary' potatoes. I dry the plants off in their containers (large bags of compost) under cover and keep the roots in them undisturbed, warm and dry, and they keep till past the New Year.

Sweet potatoes can be sliced and dried, or part-fried and frozen; they are delicious cooked in apple or pear concentrate and freeze well like that, which is easier than bottling. I guess sweet potato could be used in pickles, and as a curry base. The leaves can also be cooked and frozen as a spinach.

BELOW Sweet potatoes are easy in bags or pots under cover and crop well.

LEFT TO RIGHT Corn can be exposed and dried on the plant.
It is safer collected and kept in the dry.

SEEDS

With all these, it is their nature to want to do what we want; all we
have to do is capture their bounty. As well as pulses, celery and
pumpkin seeds already mentioned, others are well worth growing.

Poppy seeds (Papaver)

It is very easy to grow poppies: sow some poppy seeds bought for
topping breads and pastries, and some will come up. Thin them to
a foot apart for big heads. Once the plants die and wither, cut the
dried heads and keep them in a dry place till you want them. It
could not be easier. Nigella, cumin, mustard, caraway and other
seed crops can all be grown and dried in much the same way, but
need to be cut earlier and the seed heads tied in paper bags to
catch their seeds which are shed more easily.

Sunflower seeds (Helianthus)

Kids love to grow sunflowers – they are that easy. Growing loads
is also easy, but soon depletes your soil. Do not impoverish your

land unless you want them. Toasted sunflower seeds are good but
fiddly; they are really better left for the birds. As you watch the
seeds in the heads ripen, the birds rob them, so cover them with
nets, then rub off the dead flowers and ripen the heads indoors in
the warm as soon as all the seed looks full. Then they are best
broken off, cleaned, dried more and put in paper bags in tins or jars.
Left on the heads they are more likely to rot, as they absorb damp.

Sweet corn (Zea mays)

This is a major crop for starch, syrup and fodder, but we grow it for
the sweet, fresh kernels. These go off within minutes of picking,
and none tastes so good as those picked and boiled immediately.
A hungry plant, it needs full sun and a rich, moist soil. I grow early
crops under cover from late winter sowings, at one plant per
bucket; these crop by early to midsummer and are followed by
more batches in buckets, and then some in the undercover border.

The main outdoor crop can be got going sooner if you plant out
batches of plants raised indoors from mid-spring and then housed
under some temporary protection such as cloches; and then, later,
unprotected but hardened-off batches of indoor-sown plants.

pizza pancake

Make a pancake mixture as on page 92. Pour sufficient into a hot, oiled frying pan to generously coat the bottom and watch till it has just set on the top surface and turn off the heat. Quickly spread with the back of a spoon tomato purée or even sauce or ketchup, sprinkle a little oregano over this then a thick layer of grated cheese (preferably a mix of Lancashire and Cheddar and/or mozzarella), add some finely sliced onions, chopped red and green peppers, pickled nasturtium seeds and black olives. Then add a generous amount of fresh black pepper, and sometimes some dried thyme. Now put under a pre-heated grill until the top browns.

pickled nasturtium seeds

Pick and wash fresh green nasturtium seeds, brine them for a couple of days, then drain, rinse and pack in jars of spirit or cider vinegar with a few peppercorns and a bay leaf or two.

Finally, follow these with the direct-sown plants from late spring into early summer; these can make the best crops if it is sunny till late autumn. All of these are best eaten fresh, but it is better to take the lot and process them than to let them go over, as then they are wasted. More water, fish wastes and seaweed products all boost yields. Hand pollination helps under cover and early in the season.

Harvest
Look every day, pull the husk back and squeeze a kernel; if it looks like water it's too young, like cream and it's ready to take, like cheese and it's going over! If it has gone over and become tough, it is not worth processing. Tough kernels are not nice; if they are getting too chewy then give them to the wild birds, or the chickens. To dry: pull off the ear, pull the husk up away from the ear and tie it round a string or cane; keep the ears up in a dry airy space. Later, store the dried ears in a rodent-proof container.

Preserving and use
With fresh-picked cobs, boil them all as soon as possible until tender, eat the best and process the rest straight away. The blanched kernels can be scraped off the central stem and packed in cups for portions, or frozen loose and then bagged. Sweet corn can be cooked in with other dishes and makes a good sweet pickle.

You can dry sweet-corn kernels: prepare good, not overripe cobs and strip them as you would for freezing; then dry the kernels on trays in a warm, open oven for several days until totally desiccated and shrunk. These will then rehydrate overnight like beans, for use in winter dishes. You could even grind them into a rough flour; if you want to do this more, then don't grow sweet corn – different high-starch varieties are better for maize meal. The actual true popcorn can be grown, its dried seed kept and popped, but it does need a really warm summer to do well. Coloured varieties have their advocates, and are no more difficult, and the latest F1 variety is probably good. But little beats the old favourite 'Golden Bantam' when it's at its best.

Nasturtium seeds (*Tropaeolum majus*)
These are very good substitutes for capers – for sauces and for adding to pickles and pizzas. Said to be good for our lungs, they are very piquant. The leaves and the flowers can also be used in salads.

PERENNIAL VEGETABLES

These are mostly enjoyed in season. Because they are perennials, get the best stocks and enrich their soil well before planting.

Asparagus *(Asparagus officinalis)*

Plant a huge asparagus bed, with grapes overhead, and get the best, youngest plants money can buy, or sow and grow in situ and thin later – I found the variety 'Gijnlim' way outperformed all others from direct sowing. Plants need to be well fed and well spaced, about a stride either way being the minimum; the plants may look tiny now but in a few years good crowns get huge. However, you can plant twice as many and then ruthlessly crop every other for the first few years, to extinction, leaving the others to grow on strengthened. Surplus plants can be dug in autumn, potted up and forced in warm, dark, damp places for extra early spears. Putting black plastic sheet over sticks over crowns can bring on very early spears, and ordinary cloches, early ones. Always cut every shoot and process them all if not wanted straight away. Although you should not cut once summer has started, it is possible with strong crowns – if you are ruthless and care not for next year's crop – to cut them down and get a flush of strong young shoots. Fresh raw spears are sweet, and I eat them straight away; after an hour or two they are sad by comparison. Never stand asparagus in water to keep, as this ruins the flavour.

Harvest

I cut the spears off with abandon, leaving a wee stub so I can tell how a crown is doing; towards the end of the season I make sure each has five strong shoots, but I take all others till then. Do not leave wee thin spears – sprue – as this stops other buds breaking.

Preserving and use

A luxury, asparagus is rarely in surplus till late in the season; however, the water it is boiled in, with any spare and any sprue, and small spears, can be boiled and then passed through a sieve to make a soup base for freezing. The spears freeze quite well once blanched, and are best packed in brine or butter; if frozen open and bagged, many will break. Asparagus is one of the few veg that people bother to bottle, in brine and pressure treated, as it is so loved.

OPPOSITE TOP LEFT CLOCKWISE A good bunch. The tall shoots should have been cut, but are now too far gone, the bottom three are ready now. Stood upright in a tall pan for steaming.

artichoke pâté

Boil globe artichokes in salted water until the stalk end is easily penetrated with a knife. Cool and clean the hearts of the choke and scales. Pass the hearts through a sieve to get a paste. Meanwhile caramelise finely chopped onions in butter with some pepper and salt, a bay leaf and a pinch each of oregano, thyme and summer savory. Once the onions are softened, pass them through the sieve. Mix the onion paste with the artichoke paste and about a third of their total weight of fine breadcrumbs. Press the mixture into a pie dish, put a generous lump of butter on top and a lid or foil cover, then bake for an hour in the bottom of a medium oven. Cool and serve with toast or a salad.

Globe artichokes (*Cynara cardunculus Scolymus* Group)

This is one of the few crops that can be successfully grown in the ornamental border and crop there. As they are large plants, these are often relegated to corners where they get neglected, but well fed and watered they give huge, succulent heads. Ideally, get off-sets of good plants, as seed gives odd results, and plant them two strides apart each way. Keep them mulched and always remove flowers before they open, as they stop others forming.

Harvest

The first flower buds may come in late spring, although early to midsummer is more usual; the first, if removed, are followed by smaller side buds from lower down, giving more small crops. Remove them before the green bracts open wide and the purple flowery choke appears. The younger the better. Using secateurs, cut off the buds with a fingertip length of stalk, soak in brine for an hour to evict any lurking earwigs and aphids, then boil till tender in the heart. The outer bracts and the choke can be discarded and the tender heart eaten with butter, mayonnaise or other sauces. Or hearts can be pickled, often with sweet peppers, onions, garlic and other tasty things useful as starters. A real glut allows the hearts to be made into pâté, which rivals the meaty ones in savour.

Seakale (*Crambe maritima*)

Rarely grown nowadays, this rather cabbage-like delicacy is only ever eaten freshly cooked – but it comes in the middle of winter when little else is about. The plants, from offsets, at a stride or more apart, are grown for several years to build up their strength and then forced in situ as with rhubarb, or the roots are packed in pots and forced in the warm dark, for succulent blanched shoots. Batches of these roots, if enough are grown, can be forced for shoots from early winter through till spring.

Rhubarb (*Rheum x hybridium*)

This often gets the poorest spot and conditions in the garden, but can still produce more than you need. Given a good virus-free clone in rich moist soil, rhubarb can make huge clumps of dark red

FROM LEFT TO RIGHT **Use pear or apple concentrate with rhubarb for more flavour. Note the 'stringy' bits left in to add their colour. Once cooked the stringy bits can be removed.**

sweet horseradish sauce

Grate the fresh root into a third of a wine glass of cider or spirit vinegar, keeping the root covered at all times, till the glass is almost two-thirds full. Or use pickled horseradish. Then add about a third as much again – or to taste – of either condensed milk, or cream mixed with a spoonful of honey. Stir in a pinch of salt and pepper and a small spoonful of yellow mustard powder. Allow to stand in the fridge for an hour or so before serving.

chunky stalks, or more often a handful of skinny tough ones. Treat it well and force it with an old dustbin, not a bucket, and you can have excellent sticks. These are, of course, traditionally turned into rhubarb crumble, which can be frozen. Rhubarb chunks, after boiling in syrup or apple/pear concentrate, freeze well. Young tender forced stalks can be bottled or even candied. Later pulls have more sugar and substance, and cook and preserve better. Rhubarb can be made into jam and jelly, often with ginger and apples; it can even be made into wine – although that can feel as though it's dissolving your teeth faster than battery acid. And too much rhubarb definitely has a laxative effect, so don't go wild – that effect is what we introduced it from China for!

Horseradish (*Amoracia rusticana*)

Not as well known as it ought to be, this should be considered a perennial crop. I grow it in the same spot year after year by simply putting an empty tub full of composted bark over the roots in alternate years. In the composted bark appear new roots, which I take to make the sauce. The sauce is best made with the autumn and winter roots, as in spring and early summer they are exhausted. The finely grated roots keep well pickled in vinegar or white rum.

WILD VEGETABLES: STINGING NETTLES (*Urtica dioica*), GOOD KING HENRY (*Chenopodium bonus-henricus*) AND DOCKS (*Rumex*)

Along with wild fruits there are often wild vegetables for the taking, and these may be even tastier and more nutritious than our cultivated ones. In the middle ages our 'weeds' chickweed, groundsel, goosefoot and cleavers were all seen as good pot herbs, though modern stomachs and constitutions may not be as comfortable with them today. Where I come from we still eat stinging-nettle tips in spring; they are delicious fried with bacon and shallots. Far more can be consumed if they are picked, boiled and sieved to a dark green spinach, which can be used as spinach or a soup base and frozen for later.

Good King Henry, is another; a weed of wet places, this produces masses of spinach-like shoots in spring, which can be eaten on their own, like asparagus, or as a spinach and frozen for later. Watercress is another; although dangerous raw, it is safe enough once boiled down to a spinach and frozen for another day. However, although they may be traditional fare I must say I found dock leaves, hop shoots and evening primrose roots unpalatable and not worth the trouble. You may find otherwise.

Bees and poultry

Two of the other good-quality items that really make all the difference to your own delicatessen are honey and eggs.

Bees are not at all difficult to keep, but fiddly, and for a proper job require you to perform certain operations regularly and in mid-afternoon on sunny days. Thus they may suit the retired and those who work from home. You do not need a garden; bees can be housed almost anywhere, from a shed to an attic – and on top of a flat roof is ideal. A hive will often bring in dozens of pounds of surplus honey a year – though you may need to give the bees some sugar in return. But bees fill whole books on their own… read one or two first!

Chickens, however, are a piece of cake. You give them food, water, a place to perch at night under cover, a nest box and a dust bath and they will provide you with fresh eggs for ten months of the year – at least while they are young. As they get old, they lay fewer but bigger eggs. The beauty of having chickens is that they convert so much garden and household waste back into high-grade food rather than it going to the compost heap. The heap does not suffer, though, as hen-worked scraps with feathers and droppings make better compost than without the hens having a go first. (And you do not need a cockerel unless you want your eggs to hatch.)

Anyway, eggs if fresh and clean keep for several weeks in a cool place – and commercially for months if you only knew it! They do not freeze or dry well, but can be kept in water-glass solution (now hard to get – it's sodium silicate) for many months. You can separate the yolks and the whites, mix each up with sugar or salt and then freeze them as ice cubes for cooking with. Or bake them into cakes and freeze those. Ducks lay even more eggs than chickens; they make a mess of every water feature, but are more garden-friendly than chickens. Geese are good grass-cutters and lay huge eggs, but these are not for most people.

And forget anything with four legs!

TOP RIGHT **A honey comb is used to remove the wax capping the cells.**
BOTTOM RIGHT **You can eat honey wax and all.**

quiche

Make a shortcrust pastry mix. Using a food processor or by hand rub 4 ounces (110g) cold butter into 7ounces (200g) plain flour. Mix one beaten egg with 2 tablespoons chilled water and mix in until the pastry just comes together. Wrap in clingfilm and rest for half an hour. Roll out on a lightly floured surface and line a fluted flan ring. Rest and chill for half an hour then 'bake blind': Cook the pastry case, lined with greaseproof paper and filled with baking beans for 10–12 minutes at 180ºC/350ºF/gas mark 4. Remove the paper and beans and cook for a further 5 minutes until a pale biscuit brown.

For the filling sauté a sliced onion and a cubed aubergine in olive oil until softened and golden. Add a couple of cloves of chopped garlic, herbs such as thyme or rosemary, a pepper, deseeded and chopped and a couple of ripe tomatoes, also roughly chopped. Cook for just a couple of minutes more then cool slightly and tip into the pastry case. Make a custard with 4 eggs and three-quaters of a pint (450ml) milk or half milk and half cream, season, add a little smoked paprika and pour into the pastry case. Arrange courgette slices on top. Cook for 35–40 minutes until just set and golden. Enjoy warm or cold.

Variation: Try onion rings caramelised in butter, herbs and grated cheese as an alternative filling.

toast topping

Boil eggs until cooked to your liking, cool under cold running water, shell and chop. Place in a bowl and mix with some chopped chives, chervil, shredded salad leaves and some finely chopped peppers or any other fresh green things you love. Mix in some grated cheese, mayonnaise, freshly ground black pepper, a dash of tomato sauce and Worcester, soy or chilli sauce to taste. Spread thickly on hot buttered toast. I love to eat this immediately whilst the eggs are still warm.

Index

Bibliography

For recipes, storing and preserving ideas I recommend looking for modern copies of:

Most of all-
Florence White (Mary Evelyn), *Good Things in England.* 1932 et al
Mrs M. Grieve, *Herbs and Vegetables in the Orchard and in the Wild* part 1: *Wild vegetables and salads and their vitamin values*, part 2: *Edible berries and nuts*, part 3: *Pickles, chutneys, ketchup and herb vinegars*, circa 1925
Mrs C.F. Leyel, *Herbal Delights; Tisanes, Syrups, Confections, Electuaries, Robs, Juleps, Vinegars and Conserves*, 1937
Mrs Beeton's All-About Cookery, any edition prior to 1940s

For t*hose with a very sweet tooth:-*
Skuse's Complete Confectioner prior to 1940

Also
Adam's Luxury and Eve's Cookery or *The Kitchen Garden* displayed 1744, ,L. Junius Moderatus Columella De Re Rustica (first century)
William Cobbett Cottage Economy 1823
Brillat-Savarin Physiology of Taste 1825
Beecher Fruits, flowers and farming 1859

For wider reading;
Sturtevant's Edible Plants of the World, ed U.P.Hedrick, 1919
Useful Plants of Great Britain, C. Pierpoint Johnson, 1862
Kent Whealy Fruit, Berry and Nut Inventory 1993
The Vegetable Finder, HDRA, 1994 and other years
The Good Fruit Guide, Lawrence D. Hills, HDRA 1984
Forsyth on Fruit trees, 1803
The Vegetable Garden, Vilmorin-Andrieux, 1885
The Orchard House, Thomas Rivers, 1859
The Miniature fruit garden, Thomas Rivers, 1860

Acknowledgements

To all the poor so and so's who have to put up with a writer and his idiosyncracies, but persevere… still it's better than digging ditches!